My Fourth Husband and Me

To Ruth,
With Love
Margaret K Armatage

Margaret Kathleen Armatage

Editor Elspeth Richmond
Book design Maureen Salmon

Note for Librarians: a cataloguing record for this book that includes Dewey Decimal
Classification and US Library of Congress numbers is available from the Library and
Archives of Canada. The complete cataloguing record can be obtained from their online
database at:
www.collectionscanada.ca/amicus/index-e.html
ISBN 1-4120-4755-2
Printed in Victoria, BC, Canada

TRAFFORD

Offices in Canada, USA, Ireland, UK and Spain
This book was published *on-demand* in cooperation with Trafford Publishing. On-demand
publishing is a unique process and service of making a book available for retail sale to the
public taking advantage of on-demand manufacturing and Internet marketing. On-demand
publishing includes promotions, retail sales, manufacturing, order fulfilment, accounting and
collecting royalties on behalf of the author.
Book sales for North America and international:
Trafford Publishing, 6E–2333 Government St.,
Victoria, BC v8t 4p4 CANADA
phone 250 383 6864 (toll-free 1 888 232 4444)
fax 250 383 6804; email to orders@trafford.com
Book sales in Europe:
Trafford Publishing (uk) Ltd., Enterprise House, Wistaston Road Business Centre,
Wistaston Road, Crewe, Cheshire cw2 7rp UNITED KINGDOM
phone 01270 251 396 (local rate 0845 230 9601)
facsimile 01270 254 983; orders.uk@trafford.com
Order online at:
www.trafford.com/robots/04-2563.html

10 9 8 7 6 5 4 3 2

Dedication

This book is dedicated to the Third and Armatage families who have always treated me as one of their own.

I am very grateful to my editor, Elspeth Richmond, for her dedication and constructive help in the telling of my story and for her invaluable help in selecting the pictures from my vast collection. Without her, I am sure, I would never have been able to complete it.

Margaret K Armatage,

West Vancouver, 2004

Contents

Foreword

I am pleased and delighted to introduce the second volume of Margaret Armatage's memoirs, *My Fourth Husband and Me*.

When I read the final copy of Volume I, I read it in *one sitting*. I was captivated by the history, the resilience, the daring, the poetry and the response to love and tragedy by my friend. It was as if she said at the end, "Can we dance now? I love to dance." Margaret had tied so much of her life together in the book, loosening a few knots that still caused her sadness or very deep pain. She refashioned rainbows that often went unseen by others. She remembered so many of the kind people who were there when she most needed compassion. Most of all she reflected on the marital relationships that truly had been for better or worse.

There was a diversity of characters in Volume I. There were two husbands who were imposters at being helpmates. There was an older brother straight out of a Dickens novel, a bad caricature of himself. There were two hero husbands in her life. Finally, there was the beautiful and talented sister who also rose like a Phoenix out of the ashes of peril.

Who among us can tell so honest a story? I would wager that Volume I is one of a kind. Pliny writes that, in ancient Rome, men would stand on street corners and say something to the effect "Give me a copper and I'll tell you a golden story." *My Four Husbands and Me* was a golden story. It was worth many coppers.

In Volume II Margaret comes full circle. She elaborates more on the years with Colin Armatage, the kind and gentle husband number four. I did not read any of the drafts of Volume II but I suspect very strongly that Margaret has shared many of its pictures with me over the years. I will disclose a few more thoughts. The serious reader must determine his or her own reasons for spending coppers to judge true value.

Many individuals are known by various trademarks. The most delightful to me of Ted Thompson's (husband number two) was his habit of walking a few blocks from his home in Northern Maine to his pharmacy. He would have a sports coat on and a hat and perhaps a sweater. Never more warmth. It might reach temperatures more than 40 degrees below zero, Fahrenheit. Yet, there was Ted, always the same, sauntering to work, oblivious of the weather, known by what he *did not wear*.

Then there was Colin, husband number four. His trademark, known far and wide by all who admired him, was what *he wore*. Colin donned his suede leather jacket when Margaret first saw him. He had his ubiquitous suede jacket on when he flew to Margaret's home in Florida. Palm trees, romance in the air, humidity, scotch, gin and tonic. And Colin, like Elvis, with his suede.

My wife and I visited Colin and Margaret in the home they were living in not long after they were married. Had I thought more about that, we might not have intruded. We had longed to attend the World's Fair in 1986. I tried well in advance to secure lodgings, even 50 to 100 miles away. Nada. When I inquired about certain hotels, I was told things like, "Oh, a Japanese gentleman leased the whole hotel three years ago." I called my newlywed friend Margaret who said, "Please come. We have plenty of room and I want you to meet Colin." I knew about Colin. What Margaret wanted to do was to show him off.

There were two important reasons for me to meet Colin. The first was inconsequential. Margaret knew I knew that. I once told to her bail out and cut any other parachutes before she jumped and not to look back. We laughed. Margaret had seen coachmen turn into mice before. Husband number three had turned into a rat despite coming from a terrific family.

Then there was reason number two. It is a Chinese custom in many families to give presents before they are earned. Margaret had said so much to me about Colin. He was nice, he was considerate; he was a wonderful companion and husband. He was this and he was that. I asked "Is this the guy in the suede jacket?"

She said, "Oh yes, he does always have that jacket." Now how was I going to live any longer if I did not personally meet such a paragon and judge him to be true by my own standards? Margaret had already given me the dessert before the meal.

Besides, many of the friends I love most dearly have trademarks; a bow tie, argyle socks, single malt whisky and so forth. Here was a knight whose shining armor was a suede coat. I had to meet him. This guy had a real trademark. He was his own copyright.

My wife and I flew into Seattle, rented a car, visited dear friends in Eastern Washington and drove up to Margaret and Colin's new home. Margaret was genuinely delighted to see us. She was accompanied by a man with a Santa Claus aura wearing a suede jacket. Margaret said, "I want you to meet Colin."

My wife and I immediately succumbed to Colin's many charms. For the next week we were toasted, feted and spiritually rejuvenated. When we played tourist, Colin was always there to pick us up, to give us a pointer in the right direction, to spare us any grief. Our visit to Expo 86 was an unqualified success. Colin was the perfect ambassador. Just as Elvis never left the building, Colin never forgot to wear his jacket.

Meanwhile, back at the house that refused to turn into a pumpkin, I had a chance to observe him. I wanted to be absolutely sure that Colin was real. I did know that I adored his suede coat. He was the real deal with that jacket. *I* would have felt *naked* had he not worn it.

I could see plainly that Margaret and Colin had so much in common. Their flowers and garden radiated in their glow. There was a lucky halo following the two of them everywhere. They had goldfish in a pond, the same variety that Margaret pampered under a waterfall in her living room in Maine. I reflected omnisciently. The flowers and goldfish tipped the scales in favor of Colin. Margaret, to put it succinctly, was the cat's meow. This time the coachman had stayed after the ball. Which is why, dear reader, you and I are here.

Dennis E. Donham, Ph.D., friend

Franklin Park, Pennsylvania

April 25, 2004

Dear Margaret,

Just a note to tell you I have read your delightful book. June told me about it so I called and had Trafford send it to me. It brought many memories of my mom, as she loved you so. I miss her so much, but as sick as that Alzheimer's had made her, I could never wish her back.

I remember the time she brought me to your house and we washed dishes for you and I held your little dog, Andre. I remember Andre the best because he used to want to sleep with my son, Bart. On night Ron, my husband, had been out to the races and Andre went to sleep on the foot of the bed and when Ron came home he wouldn't let Ron into the bed. He used to go with me in the car and he loved that as he loved Bart so. I miss those days, being with my family.

I didn't know Ted but he sure loved you and you him. You folks did a lot of traveling. I have been to some of the places you visited and found them as beautiful as you described them. I would love to go back to Hawaii.

Mom talked of you a lot. She said you were the best person she had ever worked for because you treated her so well.

I met Mrs. Thompson, Ted's mom and she was a sweetheart of a person. That was awhile ago.

Thanks for mentioning my mom in your book. I know she would have probably cried if she could have read it.

Sincerely,

Betty (Cyr) Howlett.

This letter is just one of many I received after I wrote my first book, *My Four Husbands and Me*. Betty Howlett is the daughter of Hazel, our house cleaner in Presque Isle, Maine. Hazel was much more than a house cleaner, though... she often house sat for us when we were travelling and she helped with all our parties and social events. One of the joys of writing my first book is that I continue to hear from old friends, many of whom were in my story.

In that book I told of my childhood, growing up in Invermere and New Westminster with my sister, Betty and my brother, Jack. I told about the death of both our parents when Betty and I were teenagers and about my disastrous marriage to my first husband. I recounted my experience in business for myself, running a motel in Kamloops, BC and wrote about my divorce. While some of my early memories were sad, I think I was born an optimist. I somehow knew everything would turn out for the best. I loved running the motel but gave it all up when I met and married my second husband Ted. Ours was a love affair. We travelled around the globe, bought a new home, built a summer cottage and had homes in Florida before Ted died of lung cancer. I wrote of the difficulties I had after he died, including another bad marriage. Then I met my fourth husband, Colin, and moved back to British Columbia. This book begins there.

Chapter 1

Time Travel

I can never hear that old song *I'll Take You Home Again, Kathleen* without feeling a little teary and thinking of both my mother, whom I never knew, and my stepmother. I wonder if finding themselves far from their families in England, these two women were not homesick for the old country and the families they left far behind in England when they came to Canada. I've lived in several places and had several homes. Sometimes I long to see those homes again.

In 1985, while waiting at the airport in Palm Springs for my husband Colin's arrival, a lady approached me who asked, "Are you waiting for a flight from Vancouver, too?"

I replied I was, and asked "Are you from Vancouver?"

"No," she answered, "I'm from a place you've probably never even heard of – Invermere."

"I've not only heard of it, I was born there!" I told her.

"Well," she said, "I'm waiting for my friends, the Wilders. They have lived in the area for years."

The Wilders owned the Fairmont Hot Springs Resort, not far from Invermere. My new acquaintance later invited Colin and me over to meet them. They remembered my family and wanted to know all about our lives after we left the Invermere Valley. It was hard to tell them that within fifteen years of our leaving Invermere both our parents were dead, leaving my sister Betty and I alone and penniless. We were still in school and entirely dependent on our older brother Jack, who soon gambled and drank away our home and everything in it.

"Well," my new friend said, "You seem to have survived that time pretty well," when I explained that I had homes in both West Vancouver and Palm Springs.

I agreed. I have never been one to feel sorry for myself when things go wrong. "Get up off your duff and do something," I tell myself. It usually works, perhaps because, by nature, I'm an optimist. I believe you make your own luck.

Later that year in the spring my husband Colin and I and my sister Betty and her husband, Arthur, drove up to Invermere and stayed at the Fairmont Hot Springs. The Wilders hosted a lovely party at their beautiful home on the lake, inviting a group of people from the area who remembered our parents. We had a memorable meal sent over from the hotel; baron of beef, Yorkshire pudding, roast potatoes and fresh spring vegetables from the area. It was not the first time Betty and I had been back nor would it be the last.

In the summer of 1939 my sister Betty and her first husband Gordon drove up from New Westminster to Kamloops in their brand new Chevrolet and took my first husband Jack and me to the home our father built in Invermere. I wrote in my first book that my relationship with my husband Jack was unravelling daily. By this time I dreaded being alone with him, but I welcomed any activity with others because Jack was always on his best behavior in company.

I wasn't sure how much I actually remembered about Invermere and how much I only thought I remembered because our mother and father often talked about our homestead there and we had pictures of it as well. My father, especially, was nostalgic about the beautiful valley where he tried to live his dream of becoming a successful business man and gentleman farmer, after unsuccessfully homesteading on the prairies. As we drove 200 miles north on the Big Bend Highway, Betty and I recalled some of the stories about our life there. These stories were usually about our brother Jack and his escapades. Unfortunately trouble continued to follow Jack for his whole life – a sad story of failed relationships and unhappy children. His eldest daughter, then in her fifties, took her own life in 2002.

"Maybe I should have bought an old jalopy with a rumble seat instead of a brand new car," Gordon grumbled good-naturedly as we bounced along. "I sure hope we don't get a flat tire and that this road doesn't ruin my shocks."

We planned to camp along the way and set up our tent at Mica Creek that first night. What a night that was! Every mosquito west of the Selkirks had congregated in that campsite and we swore they just lifted up the tent flap and crawled in with us. We all suspected we were camped in a mosquito hatchery. It was a relief to get up the next morning and set off again.

By the next evening we were in Radium Hot Springs, enjoying the restorative waters and soaking our mosquito bites. I thought I remembered going there with Mother and Father, all of us, my brother Jack included, enjoying the warm waters. In fact, it must have been there that I had my first hot tub experience! Now I have a hot tub out beside my swimming pool at home and I enjoy a soak every morning. I swear it keeps me limber.

Relaxed, we set off for Invermere. In the little town we asked directions, hoping our first home was still standing.

"Oh sure," an older man told us. "I know the Sellentin house well. Don't tell me you are the Sellentin girls?" he asked.

He wanted to know all about our family and was saddened to hear that both our parents were dead. He also asked about Jack. We didn't like to tell him that contact with Jack was infrequent at best. "He's living up the coast," we told him.

Our house was just as we pictured it – a tidy log home with finely crafted windows and a neat cottage garden. I could see why the early settlers had named the town Invermere, recalling England's beautiful Lake District. With the Purcell Mountains and the clear blue sky, it really was a lovely place. I wondered, once again, about the real reason our parents left the area to start life all over again in New Westminster. I suppose they must have regretted that decision because illness and the hard times of the Depression meant that life was difficult for all of us in the ensuing years.

We knocked on the door of the neat little house and were invited in by a very pleasant couple who were obviously maintaining the property with love and pride. They had two horses, several dairy cows and, as I said, a tidy perennial garden. I was sure that most of the flowers in it were planted by my father.

They too wanted to know all about our family and our lives when we lived in the house. They laughed when, as we sat and had tea and cookies with them, we told them some of the family stories. Jack setting fire to the grass and harnessing the chickens were two about which we often laughed.

"Is this your brother Jack?" one of them asked, showing a picture of a young lad standing by a contented cow they had found in a cupboard of the house.

"That's him!" we said.

Betty and I did not return to Invermere for another thirty years. When we again drove up the beautifully paved highway in my Cadillac it was for an Invermere old timers' reunion it was 1991. We were invited by the school board members who were really looking for Jack. He was five years older than I and the only one of us who actually attended school there. I phoned him and invited him to stay with me for a few days after which the five of us, Colin and I, Betty and Art and Jack would drive up to Invermere for the reunion.

The folks there made a big fuss over him which pleased him no end. None of us ever brought up the subject of his visible unhappiness after our mother died. A day or so later we drove Jack up to Paradise Mine where a friend of his still lived.

Neither Betty nor I ever saw much of Jack after we married. We still harboured some resentment for the way he behaved when our parents died. He literally sold everything in the house to pay for gambling and alcohol. I was glad, though, that I had persuaded him to attend the reunion and that Betty and I wisely kept quiet about hard feelings.

Margaret and her brother Jack

Margaret and her sister Betty in front of their childhood home in Invermere

There were still some people who remembered Father. One gentleman said "Oh, yes, I remember him well. Your father was such a skilled carpenter and gardener! You could ask him how to do anything!"

As we drove south again, down the Kettle River Valley and back to Kamloops, I started thinking about that garden in Invermere and the garden at our next home in New Westminster. Father always said that you had to have a good perennial border and we had a big one at our house there. I remember the lovely Van Fleet Roses climbing the fence. They were a gorgeous pink variety of old garden rose and very prolific. I never see them now in nurseries or catalogues, which is a shame. Dad made us learn the scientific names of all the plants just as he had done back in England.

I had never been back to our house in New Westminster until I wrote my first book, *My Four*

Husbands and Me. We wanted to have some photographs of the house for the book and we drove over there one day to take some pictures.

I went up to the door and knocked while my sister Betty and our friend Roy Summerfield waited in the car.

"Please God," I prayed. "Let there be someone home."

My prayer was answered when a woman opened the door. I asked her if she would mind if we walked around and took some shots, telling her that my sister and I lived in the house in the 1930s. She was Carla Evans, a school counsellor in New Westminster.

"Come on in," she welcomed me. "I've often hoped someone would come along who could tell me the history of my lovely old house."

I beckoned to Betty and Roy in the car and all three of us went into the kitchen. I was amazed at how little the house had changed over the years. The good bones of the garden were still very evident. The weeping willow was still there but what had happened to the fish ponds? It was not hard to visualize where they and the cold frames and greenhouse had been.

The house was very little changed. There was the stone fireplace, the little kitchen with its wood stove and a table under the window where we ate our breakfast of oatmeal porridge, brown sugar and the cream off the top of the glass milk bottles on winter mornings. The den was little changed. It was still lined with the book shelves Father built. Father and Mother were both avid readers and, in the Depression, reading library books was free entertainment.

We climbed the stairs to what had been our bedrooms, peeking into the room I shared with Betty. Standing at the window, we could still see snowcapped Mount Baker rising in the distance. Of course the big brass bed I shared with her was no longer there. In our time it had been simply furnished and there had been few toys. In fact, we didn't even have dolls to play with. The first doll I ever had was given to me after I was married by a friend I called Uncle Ben.

A few weeks after this visit Carla invited us for lunch. When we arrived we were greeted by twenty-eight people! They included Carla's family and two couples who had lived in the house before she bought it. One couple solved the mystery of the fish ponds. Afraid that their small children would fall in and drown, they filled in the ponds in and planted grass over top.

Carla even had a special cake for us. When it was time to leave I thanked her for a wonderful 'homecoming'.

Soon after, Carla's daughter wrote to me. She had not been at the luncheon but said she had read my book. Like many people, she enjoyed reading about the traveling I had done and hoped she, also, would someday visit those same places.

"I have definitely developed a desire to see the world, one day," she wrote adding that she'd like to see my photographs sometime. She concluded the letter with something very strange. She said her mother told her that her bedroom, right beside the stairs, was the one that Betty and I shared. In that room one night she had a dream, or rather a nightmare.

I saw a man on crutches standing in my doorway. I knew he should not have been there. Then when I read your book and you told about your father coming to the door of your bedroom, on crutches, after your mother died, I knew it must have been him.

I knew that man was my father.

Later, when Carla visited me in West Vancouver she encouraged me to write my second story. "You should do it, Margaret," she said. "It is a piece of British Columbia history." That is how I came to write my second book.

This past spring I went back to Invermere again on a trip through the interior of the province with my friend Roy Summerfield. I wanted to see our house once more and to visit my mother's grave. I was dismayed to discover the house is no longer there. The only thing left of the homestead was a lilac bush which I'm sure my father planted. Although the caretakers of the little rural cemetery could tell me where my mother was buried, there was nothing marking the site. I arranged to have a stone cut and engraved in her memory. I wish I had known her.

Picture of my friend Roy Summerfield at Fort Steele

Picture of the headstone I placed on my mother's grave in 2004

Chapter 2

China

Although Colin had not had the opportunity in his life to travel a great deal, he was ready to try new experiences and was enthusiastic whenever I suggested we take a trip.

In 1985, our friends Deed and Kay Saunders wanted us to join them in the fall for a month's trip to mainland China. When I told Colin about their call and asked him if he'd ever wanted to see China, he answered, "Quite honestly, no but if you would like to go we'll go, sweetie." I started looking at the guidebooks the next day. The Chinese culture was familiar to me through Vancouver's Chinatown.

Vancouver has a vibrant Chinese community with a history that goes as far back as 1880s when Chinese labourers came to build the Canadian Pacific Railway. Chinatowns were not ethnic tourist attractions back then. The Chinese in Vancouver were not permitted to buy property outside of Chinatown until the 1930s. It is a part of the city to which I always take visitors

That summer sped by with golf, gardening and trips to Whistler. It was soon time to get ready for our adventure. When we received an official letter to say that, as the guests of the Chinese Government we must not tip anyone, we knew we were on our way.

Our tour group

Colin and our guide Gina

There were just nineteen in our tour group which included nine Chinese Canadians. We were very fortunate that Gina, a young Chinese woman working for Marlin Travel, arranged our itinerary. She would also be accompanying us throughout the tour. The eldest daughter of her Chinese father's ninth wife or concubine (he had twenty-two), she was in a unique position to show us the country. She confided to us that she hoped she would have the opportunity to meet with her father in Shanghai. She explained that she had not seen him for several years. Curious, I asked her how it was that he was virtually a stranger to her. She explained that she had lost all contact with him.

After our long flight to Hong Kong via Cathay Pacific

Airways we were taken to the Regal Meridian Hotel for a good rest. It's is always fun to return to Hong Kong. It is such a dynamic city. In its dramatic setting of sea and mountains and perfect combination of the ancient 'New Territories' villages and the bustling new Central District high rises, we were soon caught up in a cosmopolitan whirl.

Our brochures told us that this tiny 391 square mile crowded outpost is one of Asia's great success stories; its adaptable industrious people making impressive economic headway against great odds. The Chinese ceded Hong Kong Island to the British in 1841 under the Nanjing Peace Treaty. Britain acquired the Kowloon Peninsula and the New Territories under later treaties.

Hong Kong's great population growth came following World War II, from about six hundred thousand people in 1945 to about five million in 1985. I believe it has about 6.4 million people as I write.

Hong Kong, whose skyline seems to change daily, thrives on trade, manufacturing, banking and tourism. Although ninety-eight percent Chinese, Hong Kong has a sizeable western population. English is widely spoken.

After a couple of day's rest in Hong Kong, we took an afternoon flight to Shanghai. Shanghai is the largest and most densely populated city in China and a favourite of western visitors. It offers the tourist a chance to see today's China with the influences of recent cultural and political history still at work. It was in Shanghai that the Communist Party was born and the Cultural Revolution took hold. It is also in Shanghai that the results of the 'Four Modernisations' and recent western influences are most evident.

We met Gina's father, Mo Ying-gui, in our hotel in Shanghai. Gina explained earlier that during the Cultural Revolution the authorities threw many of her father's beautiful things into the street and burned them. Following this he and his twenty-two wives were separated. However, the political situation had evidently changed for the better because he had his wives back. As well, he was appointed to represent mainland China as one of the twelve important dignitaries to sit on a board dealing with the return of Hong Kong to China.

Margaret and Gina proudly wearing the Canadian flag

Sadly, Gina's meeting with her father and two brothers, all members of the Communist Party, was not a success. Her father ignored her and she was heartbroken. Afterwards, in tears, she said, "I guess I just expected too much." No doubt his behaviour reflected the still prevalent attitude towards girls in China. We thought that her father was the poorer for dismissing Gina in this way and felt that he should have been proud of her achievements.

Shanghai in 1985 was a city of contrasts. It had four airports, two elevated railways, 190 research institutes, colleges and universities and 360 modern hospitals.

The city, at that time with its eleven million people, remained the centre of China's trade and industry. Approximately one half of the country's commerce passes through Shanghai by all manner and modes of transportation. Immense gantry cranes line the modern harbour to load and unload containers at fifty deepwater berths while huge railway yards facilitate the transport of products inland to many of China's cities.

Shanghai and Beijing carry on a friendly rivalry over which city is the leading cultural and education centre. The city of Shanghai supports many artistic programmes. Ballet troupes, opera companies, symphony orchestras, acrobats, puppets and a circus are all part of Shanghai's artistic life. Medical and technical training rank as high priorities in the field of education.

The Shanghai Museum of Art and History contains the finest collections in China. Exhibits include artifacts from the second millennium BCE as well as more recent examples of Chinese ceramics, pottery, painting and calligraphy.

The heart of Shanghai is the Bund. What was once the 'Wall Street' of the foreign powers in China has now been reclaimed by the Chinese. Buildings that once housed foreign banks now serve China's foreign trade corporations. The former British Consulate is now the

Seamen's Club and the former American Club is now a police station. The parks, once barred to Chinese, are now a favourite spot for young couples and a popular place for morning exercises.

Shanghai resembles New York, Paris, London and the other great cities of the world in that the entire city is an attraction, offering many delightful activities for the traveller. As we walked the bustling promenade along the Huangpu River one Sunday, we found ourselves among many people, old and young, couples holding hands and mothers and fathers out with their children. The people seemed to enjoy having their pictures taken with their children, the little ones dressed in bright colours. When we stopped to take our photographs the children gathered around me to touch my blond hair to see if it was real.

The first evening we went to see the Shanghai Acrobatic Troupe. We also went to the Children's Palace where exceptionally talented children receive specialised training in dance, music, mathematics and other disciplines.

The next day we visited the Yuyuan Gardens and the Jade Buddha Temple. The gardens are a tranquil place with lovely moon gates and many varieties of roses.

School children dancing for us

Margaret and Colin in the moon gate

According to an old saying, if you walk through a moon gate you will be very lucky.

After viewing the jade carving and carpet factories we took the train, travelling through rice paddies to Hangzhou, one of China's most scenic cities. In the West Lake's People's Commune, we visited the world-renowned Longjing tea (Dragon Well) plantation, where workers still process the high quality leaves which are harvested three times a year.

Like my English parents before me, I love a good cup of tea, brewed with boiling water in a warmed pot. When I was a child I never dreamed that one day I would visit a tea plantation. Now I was interested to learn that the Chinese have been drinking tea for thousands of years. We usually think of the Chinese drinking clear tea, which we now understand has medicinal value as an anti-oxidant as well as lowering cholesterol, but the northern Chinese, like some of us in the West, enjoy their tea with cream.

There is an old Chinese expression: "Above there is heaven, below there are Hangzhou and Suzhou", referring to the natural beauty of the two cities and the surrounding countryside. Now that travel in China is much more convenient, more and more western visitors are discovering the picturesque gardens, temples and lakeside teahouses of Hangzhou, the city across the river.

West Lake is very beautiful with formal gardens surrounding what was the residence of the Southern Sung Emperors more than a thousand years ago. Subsequent emperors built Hangzhou-style pavilions and temples all over northern China in tribute to the beauty of Hangzhou and the West Lake area.

We were fortunate to tour the city's two largest silk factories, the Hangzhou Silk, Dying and Printing Mill and the Hangzhou Brocade Factory, which employ five thousand and eighteen hundred workers respectively. In three main departments, silk reeling, weaving and printing/dyeing, there are seven hundred auto looms. Before we went to the factory we went through plantations of mulberry trees where the silk worms feed. Every year the complex turns out 220 tons of raw silk, ten million metres of silks and satins and prints and dyes; a total of thirty-five million metres. Products turned out by the complex are rich in variety and superior in quality. Although they serve a continuing domestic market these products are also sent abroad to more than seventy different countries and regions. The factory hosts thousands of tourists who come to visit and purchase famous silk products. Workers facilities in the complex include apartments, dormitories, mess halls and a medical centre. In addition a theatre, a swimming pool, a sports ground and a number of clubs have been built for the workers as well as a nursery, a kindergarten, a primary school and a middle school for their children.

Suzhou is another very beautiful city. They call it the 'Venice of the East'. We visited the Garden of the Master of the Nets and then the Humble Administrator's Garden. Built more that four hundred years ago in the Ming Dynasty, with a pond as its centre, the garden consists of pavilions, terraces, towers and halls, all uniquely simple and elegant.

Margaret has a lesson in silk making

The following day we had a boat ride down the Grand Canal from Suzhou to Wuxi. We cruised around the many scenic spots of Lake T'ai, one of China's largest lakes and then toured another workshop where they made clay figures. We watched the workers paint the figures freehand. A visit to an acupuncture school completed our day.

Margaret in the Humble Administrator's Garden

35

I must tell you more about the Grand Canal. Actually, they call it the ancient Grand Canal. That and the Great Wall are two world-famous symbols of China's ancient civilisation. Through the ages the canal has seen many changes. Today the 1,794 km long canal extends from Beijing in the north to Hangzhou in the south. It runs through the provinces of Hebei, Shandong, Jiangsu and Zhejiang linking five great rivers, namely the Haihe, Huang He (Yellow), Chang Jiang (Yangtze), Huaihe and Qiantang rivers. We saw many lovely gardens.

Travelling along the canal we got a peep into the local life. Wuxi is the centre of water transport in the Taihu Lake area. There are many small bridges, each one unique and, in consequence, many old buildings were constructed along both sides of the canal. Some even protrude out onto the water. People living there draw water up from the canal directly to their windows. There are piers just outside their doors. We saw all types of boats carrying all manner of cargo. There were so many barges and riverboats, so many in fact, you could hardly see the water between them.

Wuxi, known as the Bright Pearl beside Lake Taihu, is a city at the lower reaches of the Yangtze River. Lake Taihu is famous for

The Grand Canal

its majestic hills. The city's vegetable and fish stalls are abundant with produce from the countryside. This is the 'Land of fish and rice' or the 'Land flowing with the milk and honey of China'. Tortoise Head Gardens is a famous scenic spot where the surrounding hills rise one upon the other, all surrounded by water. Other gardens and parks include the Li Garden, Plum Garden, Xihui Park and the Jichang Garden, each in a different architectural style with its own unique layout, rivalling one another in beauty. I wanted to buy one of the little spirit houses one sees in many Chinese gardens but it would have been far too heavy to carry. However, when I returned home I was determined to build a miniature Chinese garden of my own. For his part, Colin hoped my landscaping plans were scaled down to something we could manage ourselves. I kept this in mind. Now, whenever I stand on the little bridge over the pond in my garden, I remember those lovely gardens in China and the time Colin and I shared there.

Produce for sale on an ancient city street

From Wuxi we took the train to Nanjing, both a major industrial and cultural centre, which at various times has been the capital city of China. Today it is the capital city of Jiangsu Province. Once on board the train we noticed pot bellied stoves in each car we passed through. Later our porter boiled a kettle on one of these and then served us piping hot tea in china mugs with lids. What a good idea, I thought, to keep the tea hot.

Industry in the area is comprised of coal mining, metallurgy, petroleum refining, machine tool manufacture, food processing and automobile and ship manufacturing. Large agricultural communes in the Nanjing area produce varied crops of grain, tea, vegetables, melons and other fruits. The government also takes great pride in its reforestation programme. Twenty-eight million trees had been planted since 1949 and I am sure it has doubled since we were there.

Nanjing's importance has been greatly influenced by the erection of the Yangtze River Bridge in 1968. The bridge connects Nanjing with Beijing to the north, Guangzhou to the south and Shanghai to the south east. The Chinese are justifiably proud of the Yangtze River Bridge. Completed in 1968 after ten years work, the Chinese undertook the job themselves only after engineers from the Soviet Union could not surmount the swirling seventy foot deep waters and bedrock floor. And what a bridge it is! We crossed it several times. Below us the Yangtze River seemed huge.

One evening in Nanjing we had dinner at the top of a skyscraper with a revolving restaurant. Because it was my birthday Colin put a silver dollar on the sill and it came back with more coins along with it!

After a tour of the Jiangsu Museum, with its extensive collection of jade, we continued on to the Dr. Sun Yat-sen Mausoleum and the tomb of the first Ming Dynasty Emperor. Those of us in the tour from the Vancouver area were familiar with the name of Dr. Sun Yat-sen. There is a very lovely memorial garden in the heart of Vancouver's China Town honouring him. He gave up his medical career to work for political reform in China in the 1890s. His ideals were summarized in the Three Principles of the People – nationalism, democracy and the people's well-being. He and his followers were determined to overthrow the corrupt Manchu regime. He spent the rest of his life working to unite the many feuding groups within China.

Later we visited the Zijin Shan Mountain Observatory; China's third largest, built in 1985.

The following day we flew to the ancient city of Xian, once an artistic Mecca, and the capital of eleven dynasties. At the top of the 'must see' list Gina said, was the Banpo Village, the site of a Neolithic community dating back to 6000 BCE. We spent a whole day touring the Qin Shi Huang Tomb, a fantastic display of the life-like terracotta warriors and horses that was unearthed in 1974. While sinking wells for farmland irrigation construction, members of a commune stumbled on this funeral pit containing a terracotta army. In order to display this outstanding discovery in its original condition, it has not been moved. Instead, the whole pit has been encompassed under a seven-metre single spanned roof. The building is 230 metres long and covers 16,000 square metres.

The Banpo Museum is filled with very early writings, also old stone articles and bone tools. The Forest of Steles, in the Shaanxi Provincial Museum, has six exhibition rooms and five galleries displaying more than seventeen hundred kinds of rare steles, upright stone slabs or pillars bearing an inscription of a family history, dating from the Han Dynasty.

Overwhelmed and with heads spinning from all the sights Gina arranged for us, we flew from the ancient capital to the present capital, Beijing, the second largest city in China. First we were taken to the famous Tiananmen Square and next to The Forbidden City or the Palace Museum, as the authorities insist on calling it. A few years later, in 1989, we would see on television the massacre in Tiananmen Square, remembering the beautiful ancient city and the many lively young people we had seen there. I couldn't help thinking then of Dr. Sun Yat-sen and his noble attempts to bring democracy to the country.

We saw the extensive reconstruction of the Summer Palace which occupies 290 hectares. It used to be the Imperial Gardens of the Qing Dynasty. After the palace burned down in 1880 it was rebuilt in 1888 by the Empress Dowager Cixi at great expense using money originally appropriated for building a Chinese navy.

The Temple of Heaven, a geometric masterpiece of thirteenth century architecture, and steeped in the historic majesty of the Summer Palace was next on the very full itinerary through which Gina guided our little group. Later in the afternoon we saw the Ming Tombs, the burial site of thirteen of the sixteen Ming Dynasty Emperors.

At the end of each sight-filled day in Beijing we were always glad to return to our suite in the Great Wall Hotel, with its two bathrooms, a bar and four telephones! Both Colin and I were very tired each evening and had no trouble falling asleep as soon as our heads hit our pillows. One night I remember him saying, "You asked if I wanted to see China. We are seeing it!"

The next day we put on all our clothes and bought more to layer on top. It had turned very cold and we were going to climb part of the Great Wall. We even bought Russian style fur hats. I was very glad I had packed my rain and wind proof golf suit. Layering is certainly the way to go.

We climbed quite a way up to a tower on the Great Wall which is six thousand kilometres, running from Kansu province to Hopeh province along the southern edge of the Mongolian plain. It ranks among the greatest ancient projects in human history. Badaling near Beijing, which includes the important Jujongguan Pass, is the most magnificent section of the wall. What a thrill it was to walk on this Great Wall I had heard so much about. But, as it was very cold and snow-covered in spots it was also good to return to our warm bus.

Margaret and Colin on the Great Wall – layering is the way to go

A crowd watches Margaret and Colin on a camel near the Great Wall

Margaret and Gina with some Chinese Army officers on the Great Wall

One of the faces of China

It took us ages to go through the Palace Museum of the Forbidden City. In the old days it was the permanent residence of the emperors of the Ming and Qing Dynasties. A total of twenty-four emperors lived here and exercised supreme feudal autocratic power over the country. The Imperial Palace covers an area of about 720,000 square metres including 9,000 compartments with a total floor space of 150,000 square metres. The main buildings are the three great halls: the Hall of Great Harmony, the Hall of Middle Harmony and the Hall of Preserving Harmony. In the outer court are the three palaces: the Palace of Heavenly Purity, the Hall of Union and the Palace of Earthly Tranquillity; and in the inner court are the six east and six west palaces. It is the largest most magnificent and most complete complex of ancient Chinese architecture. What a place!

No visit to Beijing would be complete without a visit to the very large zoo. Of course we saw the panda bears and babies. We also became very lost and no one spoke any English. I was glad that there were six of us together and Gina did keep the bus waiting for us. I do hate to be late and keep others waiting but we really could not find our way out. Colin remained calm, saying he was pretty certain the bus would not leave without six of us.

The last night in Beijing we went to a famous Peking duck restaurant. I must say the duck was very tasty, but there was just not enough of it.

Margaret on the Li River, Guilin

The solitary summits of Guilin

We flew to Guilin, a city of unparalleled beauty. Our trip down the tranquil Li River was something I will never forget, with rock hills in a myriad of forms rising straight out of the water, some graceful, others grotesque. The river was like glass and the reflection of the hills, bamboo groves and the mist-shrouded crags have inspired painters and poets for many centuries.

Guilin is so different from any place that I have seen. According to geological surveys the area was originally a vast expanse of sea. As a result of repeated shifting of the earth's crust, the limestone once on the sea bed, rose

44

and became layered. With erosion, the limestone weathered into peaks, solitary summits, underground rivers and caves. We went into quite a few caves: the Reed Flute Cave, the Seven Star Cave and quite a few others. We also saw the Forest of Stone Tablets.

"Watch for the fishermen with their cormorants," Gina informed us. "They have been fishing in this unique way for centuries."

The birds dive for fish which they cannot swallow because of metal rings around their necks. The fishermen pull on ropes tied to the rings and take the fish from the birds. At last, at the end of day, the birds are allowed to dine on their catch.

We left this lovely spot reluctantly as we were staying in a very beautiful garden hotel. What a contrast awaited us as we flew to the boisterous atmosphere of Guangzhou, long known in the West as Canton. It is the southernmost metropolis in China.

Guangzhou is one of the few cities that remained accessible to foreign visitors after 1949. The Chinese Export Commodities Fair attracts fifty thousand foreign business representatives each year. For this reason, Guangzhou had longer exposure to Western fashions and consumerism.

I read that legend has it that Guangzhou was founded by five heavenly beings who descended to earth astride five goats. We saw a statue of the five goats near the entrance to Yuexiu Park, each animal bearing a stalk of rice in its mouth. The rice was the symbol of the promise that the region's population would never suffer from famine.

This city teems with factories, about four thousand we were told. It was the starting point of the Silk Road on the sea.

We returned to Hong Kong by express train, travelling past the horrible barbed wire fence that separated Hong Kong from China. On our last day in Hong Kong, we drove to the Peak to see the view, the harbour and the high rises. That evening, a terrific farewell dinner ended our trip to China.

"Well," said Colin as we settled into our seats on the Cathay Pacific plane for our trip home, "We did see China!"

Chapter 3

Expo 86

When we arrived back in Vancouver in November, Betty and Art met us at the airport with umbrellas. As we drove home along the glistening streets, windshield wipers going full tilt, we knew we were home at last, heads full of the images of ancient China, eager to develop our pictures and relive the trip in front of the fire.

Newcomers to Vancouver often find the rainy winters depressing and I must admit that I looked forward to escaping to a sunnier climate for a few weeks after Christmas, when what we call the 'winter blahs' set in. Colin and I both also looked forward to a trip in my new car, a beautiful bronze Cadillac with maroon leather seats. We drove south to our home in Palm Desert after spending Christmas day with my sister Betty and her husband Art and set off early on Boxing Day. Christmas Day had been sunny; Boxing Day was wet and dreary. I remember saying to Colin, "I love this car! I think it's the prettiest one I've ever owned."

"And how many would that be, Sweetie?" he asked.

47

"I'm not sure," I laughed. "I've lost count."

We were in for a surprise. At the border crossing near Blaine, Washington, a very officious customs officer ordered me out of the car, into an office. I looked around nervously and probably looking guilty as well, wondering what I had done to be singled out in this way. Colin, who had been allowed to come in with me, looked concerned while trying to reassure me.

"I'm sure it's nothing," he said.

I thought back to our recent trip to China, wondering if the customs and immigration authorities thought that I had smuggled something illegal into the country. But, no, that couldn't have been the problem. Ted once said, "Don't ever do anything illegal, hon. Anyone could tell in a minute if you were up to something, just by looking at your face."

I remembered the time an Irish couple we had met in South Africa asked Ted to take a rather large sum of money out of the country for them. Of course, he refused. I was glad that he waited until later to tell me about it.

I've always made it a practice to be totally honest all my life and couldn't think why I should be sitting there waiting like someone who had committed a felony. I soon found out.

Since my marriage to Ted I had lived in the US with

a green card. I was not a US citizen and had never surrendered my Canadian citizenship.

"You have been absent from the country for more than six months," the official informed me. "I'm afraid you will either have to return to Canada or surrender your green card right now. Then we can allow you to enter the country as a Canadian tourist. Otherwise you are not going anywhere else unless it's in front of a judge."

So that was how I came to surrender the card I had since 1955 – for almost 30 years since my marriage to Ted. Thank heavens I had it with me. All of a sudden it felt as if I was severing myself from my past life with him. I was close to tears.

Colin put his arm around me and that almost made it worse. I was determined not to cry in front of the officer. We literally had to turn around and re-enter Canada.

"I'm sure we'll get this straightened out," Colin assured me, as we walked back across the border.

The Canadian customs men were very nice and said they were glad to have me back, and so soon! Then Colin turned the car around once more and I entered the US for the first time in many years as a Canadian citizen.

Four hours later we were on our way again. Stopping in the afternoon at our favourite restaurant in Eugene, Oregon, we told our waitress about the ordeal. She brought us each a cocktail and didn't charge us for them. I have often thought about this experience, especially in the last two years since the 911 tragedy. While the American government can be pretty difficult, its citizens are some of the friendliest anywhere.

We arrived back at our home at the Chapparal Country Club in time to get dressed up, Colin in his tuxedo and me in an elegant long dress, for the New Year's Ball.

A picnic at Palm Desert

Margaret and Colin dressed for a party at the Chapparal Country Club

We bought our house there in 1983 and finally sold it in 1992. Facing the 13th green on the golf course it had a spacious living and dining room, three bedrooms and a patio with lovely jacaranda trees. We had access to a swimming pool and, naturally, to the golf course.

The desert was spectacular that spring, with cactus blooms and the mountains in the distance, and soon we were playing host to friends and family eager to flee the January weather back home. One attraction visitors enjoyed was the White Water picnic area where children could fish for trout – all the more fun because we always returned home and had fresh fish for supper. We often barbecued our catch or some steaks and if we didn't feel like cooking we would eat out at one of the Desert's restaurants.

Betty, Art and Margaret golfing in Palm Desert

We always headed for home in April, knowing that, even if it was raining there, the days would be warmer and everything in the garden would be running wild, especially the forsythia. It was one of the things that I had missed, living on the eastern seaboard in Maine, where the winters were harsher and spring so much later in coming. Often it seemed as if spring lasted just a few short days before the heat of summer.

April, 1986, was a very special year for the city and people of Vancouver. It was the year of the World's Fair, Expo 86, and it turned out to be a year like no other. It was a fair to be remembered proudly by all of us who were lucky to be living here then.

Knowing we would be sure to have many friends

visiting us that summer, we bought passes for the entire time. It was much more economical than paying individually each time we went. I think this was a very clever marketing strategy because it ensured good attendance by local people now committed to visiting often. These people became the fair's biggest boosters and the fair was a financial success as a result.

We also had passports for the season which were stamped by each of the international and Canadian pavilions and made an attractive souvenir of the event. We took in most of the great entertainment from the different countries.

One of the things I remember best about Expo was the fun of looking forward to it. It was so well and attractively advertised that most Vancouverites could hardly wait for it to begin. Jimmy Pattison, a well-known local business man, masterminded the whole affair and from the opening day celebrations to the final fireworks display, it never failed to live up to our expectations.

Everyone said that Jimmy Pattison put Vancouver on the map. People came from all over the world, celebrities like Prince Charles and Princess Diana, who made headlines because she fainted, and talented performers such as Harry Belafonte whom I met back in the 50's, and many troupes of musicians and acrobats. Every day was new and exciting.

The exposition's planners insisted on a high quality

for everything, including the food available. From the snack bars right up to the expensive restaurants there were opportunities to sample a variety of foods from many parts of the world. There was barbecued salmon and bannock served by the region's native peoples, good old fashioned prairie cooking at the restaurant at the Saskatchewan Pavilion, elegant wiener schnitzel and sparkling wine at the Austrian. There was also a VIP lounge and restaurant where we entertained important visitors. The event gave Canada and all the provinces, as well as many other countries from around the world, an opportunity to display their best artists, attractions and products.

Every evening ended with spectacular fireworks. We left with a feeling of pride in our country and our people.

Many people in the city, including my stepson and daughter, Dennis and Mary, responded to a request from the Expo Committee asking Vancouverites to host visitors and turn their homes into bed and breakfast accommodation. Dennis and Mary had a cabin cruiser which enabled them to show their guests some of our spectacular coastal scenery as well as a view of the cityscape, especially lovely at night. People who did this met people from all over the world and have kept up these friendships, even though the event was 18 years ago.

Our visitors, some from as far away as England, included my old friend Dennis Donham who wrote the introduction to my first book, *My Four Husbands and Me*, as well as this one.

Chapter 4

There'll Always be an England

Just a few weeks ago I received a letter from Her Majesty, Queen Elizabeth and no, I'm not 100 or even 90. It came about this way. I was responding to a notice in *This England* magazine, the beautifully illustrated 'patriotic quarterly for all who love our green and pleasant land'. The publisher asked readers to write to Her Majesty to ask her to withhold royal assent from Parliament's decision to adopt the Euro. I wrote my letter and thought to myself, "Why not send her a copy of my book along with it?"

Why not indeed! It has always been my philosophy to act on a well-considered impulse. Without that attitude I would never have married Ted, my second husband and had the one great love affair of my life. I would never have entered the motel business, travelled around the world on my own or written a book. And yes, I would never have married my first husband Jack and endured almost fourteen years in an abusive relationship, or married my third husband Lou, another disaster. That leads me to another piece of hard-earned wisdom which is that some things in this world don't turn out right or even for the best. Things do go wrong. I learned that early enough when my parents died in the Depression when my sister Betty and I were really just kids. It was reinforced when Ted died of lung cancer far too young and when Colin died a few short years after our marriage. I know that when I see my sister, Betty, a victim of Alzheimer's. "Why her and not me?" I've often wondered. However, when things go very wrong in your life and you are the survivor you must, as the songs says, 'pick yourself up, dust yourself off and start all over again'.

But to return to my letter to the Queen. I actually received a reply from Her Majesty thanking me for sending a copy of my book to her. Seeing the Buckingham Palace stationary brought back a flood of memories. I remember the thrill of my first 'royal' experience. Ted and I were staying at the Lord Beaverbrook Hotel in Fredericton. We were in the lobby when the elevator door opened and there, not more than a few feet away, were Queen Elizabeth and Prince Phillip. Everyone in the lobby, quite a crowd, suddenly surged forward.

"Hold your ground!" Ted instructed me.

There were two little boys in kilts in front of Queen Elizabeth and she bent down and shook hands with them. I suppose she must have been thinking of her own little boys, Princes Charles, Andrew and Edward, who looked so charming in their kilts.

The Queen wore a tiara and what seemed like a million emeralds. Her smile and beautiful complexion were dazzling. Prince Phillip was very handsome, as well. As they proceeded through the lobby, the skirt of the Queen's beautiful ball gown brushed mine. I was thrilled!

I've always believed the Queen plays an important role in Britain. As the head of state she can entertain important visitors and, within the Commonwealth, she provides an opportunity for its members to meet in a neutral setting.

Of course, both my parents were English and brought us up to have a healthy respect for the monarchy. We had a complete set of books about the 'home' country, as Mother and Father called it, and its history, illustrated with many pictures. Betty and I would often get the books down from the book shelves my father built and stretch out on the floor, pouring over them for hours. These books mysteriously disappeared after our parents died. I guess Betty and I realized that our brother Jack sold them out from under us to pay for liquor. From them, I already knew the Tower of London, the Beefeaters, the bridges across the Thames and the swans in the parks. As well, like every school child in Canada at that time, we could recite with ease, every king and queen from Egbert and Aethewulf down through all the Henrys and their wives and on to Queen Victoria, King George V and Queen Mary. Had my parents lived through the abdication of Edward VIII I don't know what they would have thought, and of course, the scandals of the present Royal family would have been unthinkable to them.

Ted and I spent a wonderful holiday in England not long after we married, when we travelled to Switzerland to attend a Rotary International convention. I felt as if I were in some sense returning home the first time I visited England. "I really am in England!" I thought. I felt so proud when Ted and I stood in the crowd outside Buckingham Palace watching the changing of the guard. If only Father had been more successful, I couldn't help thinking. How proud he would have been to return to the country of his birth. And while neither he nor my stepmother realized their dream of returning to their homeland, they certainly instilled in us a strong sense of our 'Englishness'.

Looking back, after the busy Expo 86 season and all our visitors, I can't believe Colin and I really headed off to England at the end of August. We may have been the only people leaving Vancouver because most Vancouverites chose to stay home and be tourists in their own home town that year. Nevertheless, leave we did, for a three week grand tour of Great Britain.

Like every woman traveller I give quite a bit of thought to what to pack for a holiday. If there's any possibility that I might have to carry any of my luggage I'll limit myself to what I can fit into my suitcase on wheels and my overnight bag. It's a good idea to pack a change of wash and wear undies, a blouse and socks.

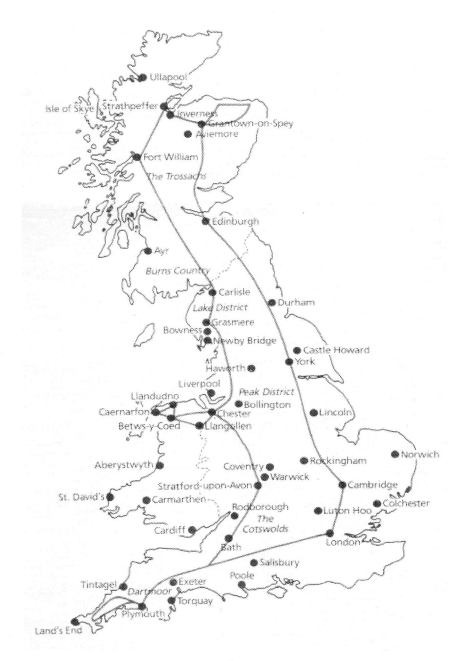

Grand Tour of Britain map

That way, if your luggage doesn't arrive when you do, you can survive until it catches up. I take good, comfortable flat shoes. My Wallabys are perfect and never wear out. I never wear sneakers because I have discovered that people think you are an American if you wear them. I take a good basic black dress, slacks, a sweater or two and washable shirts. I try to keep everything to one colour so I can co-ordinate outfits. I take two hand bags, one for evening and a larger one for daytime use which has to hold all my travel documents such as my passport, tickets, traveller's cheques and cash. It is a good idea to have a purse with pockets so you can keep your things separate. Theft is a problem all over the world now, and nothing sets you apart as a tourist more than standing around rifling through your bag.

Colin and I shared enthusiasm for many things and he was learning to enjoy travelling as much as I did. As our plane began its decent over Heathrow I was as excited as I had been on my first trip to England with Ted. Now I would have the fun of showing all the sights to Colin. He, like Ted, was a reader and before we left on this trip he did quite a bit of research.

As soon as we were through customs and immigration we took one of London's famous taxis to our beautiful hotel in Mayfair. Mayfair was one of the most fashionable addresses in the city and still makes me think of Noel Coward and Gertrude Lawrence. Everyone is 'terribly smart'.

Taxi drivers in London are among the most knowledgeable in the world, having to pass stringent exams on the city's streets and buildings. Of course, the first thing you notice is that the cabbie is driving on the 'wrong' side of the road. It takes some getting used to and I felt good about our decision not to rent a car this time. We would soon be on a comfortable coach, letting someone else navigate and deal with the traffic. In the meantime, we had two full days in London to enjoy.

We rested that first day, making ourselves stay awake until our inner clocks were set to UK time. That first afternoon we enjoyed a room service tea. The Earl Grey arrived in a lovely china pot with a silver pitcher of hot water. As we sipped our tea from china cups and enjoyed floury scones with strawberry preserves, clotted cream and raspberries, it really did feel as if I had returned home. The room, with its comfortable slip-covered chairs, cozy bedspreads and drapes, all in a pattern of violet nosegays, seemed perfect in every way. The $90 cost of the room seems very reasonable today when you can easily spend upwards of $350 a day for something not nearly so convenient and lovely.

Refreshed, we strolled over to Harrod's. I could see that England was now as ethnically diversified as Canada and there were motor bikes everywhere.

The next day we were up bright and early and after a typical English breakfast of eggs, bacon, fried tomatoes and toast, we toured the high spots of the city in one of the bright red, open aired double-decker buses. The city had a festive air because the streets were being decorated for the wedding of Sarah Ferguson and Prince Andrew.

One of London's fashionable streets decorated for the wedding of Prince Andrew to Sarah Ferguson

We went to Westminster Abbey and the Tower Bridge to see the crown jewels and Big Ben. If I was feeling guilty about the amount of food we had eaten at breakfast, I was soon glad that we had fortified ourselves for the walking we did at every stop. The weather couldn't have been better and we used our umbrellas only once when it poured on our last day.

On our second day we went to Hampton Court where a guide in period costume told us the history of the palace. It was originally built for Cardinal Wolsey, but upon his downfall, became the property of Henry VIII. It was here that Anne Boleyn lived with Henry. When I saw the great kitchen I tried to imagine all the cooks, scullery maids and servers rushing to feed the royal entourage. When you consider the number of people beheaded, burned at the stake or hung, drawn and quartered at the time, below the stairs was most likely the safest place to be unless you burned the wild boar turning on the great spit.

The lovely formal gardens, English, French and Italian were then, as now, places of rest and refuge as well as rendezvous. There is also an ancient maze which made me a little nervous. The many different chimney pots entranced Colin.

The following day we left on what was billed as the Grand Tour of Britain. We clambered aboard a bus to Salisbury.

The British Isles feel like home

Bus tours are a very good way to see the English countryside, especially for first time travellers and for singles. They take away the stress related problems of finding places to stay every evening as well as finding places to eat. Another feature in their favour in Great Britain, of course, is the fact that one doesn't have to do the driving. Our tour had both a driver and a tour guide. By late in the afternoon, when we arrived at the beautiful Salisbury Cathedral, we had introduced ourselves to the rest of the group and were feeling comfortable with the prospect of spending the next two weeks in close proximity.

Since we were in Salisbury, scaffolding has been erected to repair the highest spire in England, built by successive generations of local craftsmen. Graceful Georgian houses surrounded the Cathedral Close where Handel lived at one time.

The next day our tour took us through the beautiful countryside of Devon and I marvelled once again how much of England is still very rural. We later stayed in Plymouth in the Mayflower Hotel, the name reminding us that the Pilgrims left for the New World from Plymouth in 1620. Sir Francis Drake also set off from Plymouth to defeat the Spanish Armada. It felt good to stretch our legs on a walk through the town, crossing a bridge built by Brunel, a great English engineer, in 1857.

We later looked across the water to St. Michael's Mount in Cornwall, then toured St. Ives, and saw another great cathedral, Truro. From the bus we saw many abandoned Cornish tin mines, remembering an old verse that began, 'Jesus was a tin man' – a reference to the belief that Jesus visited Cornwall at some time. This is not as far-fetched as might seem, because many ships from the Mediterranean did visit the south coast of Britain around that time to trade. When you see many dark-haired and dark-eyed people in the southern coastal areas of England, you realize that it is quite possible that many of them have Mediterranean ancestry.

There had been a hint of fall in the mornings the first few days we were in England but our next stop was the Cornish Riviera where the weather was almost tropical. Palm trees added to the illusion. By lunch time we were always ready for a pub lunch and of course, in Cornwall, the best pub lunch is a Cornish pastie washed down with mugs of cider or ale. I reminded myself that it's not wise to drink ale or cider with your lunch if you want to be alert for the afternoon's sightseeing. We generally waited until the evening to enjoy a pre-dinner drink.

Our next stop, Bath, is a city of lovely Georgian terraces. The Roman baths, called *Aquae Solis* or waters of the sun, lay buried for centuries before they were rediscovered by in the 18th Century. Beau Nash, the arbiter of fashion at the time, and the architects Woods and Son, transformed the city, making it an attractive spa for wealthy aristocrats during the reign of George III and the Regency period. The wonderful films adapted from the novels of Jane Austen bring to life the fashions of that period. Sadly, the elegant Beau Nash died in poverty, a victim of his gambling addiction. The baths receive half a million gallons per day of water at a constant temperature of 49°C.

We continued our tour through the Cotswold's to the lovely town of Broadway, where I had stayed before with Ted, then on to Stratford-upon-Avon where, this time, we stayed at the Arden Hotel. We had plenty of time to see all the famous places: the Royal Shakespeare Theatre on the river Avon, Shakespeare's birthplace and the church where he is buried. We then went to the village of Shottery to see Anne Hathaway's Cottage.

Stratford has been a village since the Bronze Age, but its prosperity has been due, in a large measure, to the fact that William Shakespeare was born there on the 23rd of April, 1564. Ted and I saw *Romeo and Juliet* the first time I visited the town but this time there were too few hours to see a play.

One of the drawbacks of taking a tour like ours was the fact that often, if we'd been driving ourselves, we could have attended a play or concert or stayed as long as we liked in one of the historic buildings or lovely towns. Being on a tour also means you are up and about early in the morning, sometimes a bit demanding, agreed, but, on the other hand, it assures that you don't miss important sites. It was very pleasant being on the bus with Colin. He was an agreeable companion and, as a result, didn't mind some 'companionable silences'. We shared a love of gardens, too, and England has the best.

The Rows in Chester

Outdoor biffies, Chester

"Walking the wall which surrounds the city of Chester is a must," I told Colin as we approached it. It is a two mile circular walk and the only completely walled town in Britain. There is so much to see from it. We could see the medieval castle started by the Romans before they withdrew from Britain at the beginning of the fifth century. You can also see galleried tiers of shops known as the Rows. It was fun to browse without being rushed and, had it been a wet day, sheltered from the rain. It brought back happy memories of my previous visit to the city.

This time Colin and I walked along the river Dee and took pictures of the lovely formal gardens. One of the town's most charming features is the many Elizabethan, half-timbered black and white buildings.

From Chester we toured North Wales, visiting Llangollen, a very clean market town. Musical festivals are held here including the celebrated International Eisteddfod. In fact, I think throughout the world, Welsh expatriates gather to sing and to keep their culture alive. Where I live, in Vancouver, there is a Welsh men's choir and a Welsh society.

Crossing the Menai Bridge over the Menai Straits, we went on to Caernarfon Castle, perhaps best known now as the site of the investiture of the Prince of Wales in 1969. The castle was built between 1285 and 1322. The castle overshadows the market town completely. The question of Welsh loyalty to the British crown and government is not new. Many Welsh nationalists, like those in Scotland, do not consider themselves British and strive to keep their language as a statement of this fact. The first Prince of Wales, Edward in 1301, was so named to placate the Welsh, who resisted English rule.

Margaret in Snowdonia

Back on the bus, we left the castle town and headed over the Cambrian Mountains. We passed many mountain streams and went through Llanberis Pass. We had a great view of Snowdon, the highest mountain in Wales, 3560 feet above sea level. Everywhere we looked there were sheep, many different breeds, and peaceful lush green valleys. This

Colin and the 'walking sweaters' in Wales

area is the centre of the woollen industry. They call the sheep 'walking sweaters'. That afternoon we stopped at the village of Betws-y-Coed, possibly the loveliest village in Wales.

The next morning we headed back to England and north to the beautiful Lake District. We visited Windermere, Ambleside and Grasmere, where Wordsworth lived. We also visited the town of Denbigh. Here in a small cottage, H. M. Stanley, of "Dr. Livingstone, I presume?" was born. We stopped for lunch at the Priory Tavern in an old churchyard.

Lake Windermere is beautiful with many lovely homes around it. In the early fall many of the deciduous trees were turning colour and reflected in the calm water. Nearby we saw the smallest house in England, built on a bridge. I wondered if my father expected Invermere, where he settled in BC, to be much like the Lake District.

Leaving Keswick at the top of Derwentwater in the midst of beautiful mountain scenery, we entered Scotland through Gretna Green and the 'bonnie banks' of Loch Lomond. Travelling over the pass of Glencoe to Fort William at the foot of Ben Nevis I remembered the first time I entered England in 1957, crossing the Scottish border and seeing a sign which read 'England/Scotland'. This time we saw many red deer before pulling into a distillery, the home of Ballantine Scotch Whisky.

We travelled the full length of Loch Lomond, passing farms with long-haired Scottish cattle grazing contentedly and many small waterfalls along the way to Glencoe.

Glencoe is beautiful but a haunting sadness prevails the site of the terrible massacre of the MacDonald clan by soldiers of the Campbell clan in February, 1692. Our guide explained that over the preceding two centuries disputes had flared up periodically between these two, the MacDonalds the rebels, and the Campbells representing the English authority. Ordered to take an oath of allegiance to the English king, William II, the chief of the MacDonald clan did so reluctantly but too late to prevent the tragedy about to unfold.

On February 1, 1692, Captain Robert Campbell received orders to murder every MacDonald male under the age of 70. Campbell, who had grudges against the MacDonalds, was not reluctant to order his men to carry out these orders. What made the crime so heinous was that his men were quartered with unsuspecting MacDonald clansmen. Forty men were massacred in their beds before dawn. While some of the MacDonald men managed to escape to the hills, most died of exposure and hunger.

Scotland is a land of lakes. On our trip we passed many of the loveliest, including Loch Linnhe, Loch Lochy, Loch Garry and Loch Loyne. We saw the ruins of Invergarry Castle, once the seat of the MacDonalds of Glengarry, where we saw the lock working and thought that sometime it might be fun to take a boat through the waterways. There are about twelve locks in what they call the Neptune Ladder.

Margaret in front of the Highland Hotel

We travelled through some of the finest Highland scenery around Glen Shiel and through the village of Invershiel to reach Dornie. Nearby the village, in the waters of Loch Duich, lies probably the most photographed castle after Edinburgh Castle – Eilean Donan. It dates from the Middle Ages, but was reduced to a ruin in 1719 while it was garrisoned by Spanish troops when they faced attack by three English men o'war. We remembered the swarthy people we'd seen in Cornwall and fully expected to see more of them this far north.

That night as we climbed between soft and cosy comforters at the Highland Hotel we were excited to think the next day we'd be going 'over the sea to Skye', home of the MacDonald Clan.

It was to Skye that the 'Young Pretender', Bonnie Prince Charlie, dressed as a woman, fled aided by Flora MacDonald. Our guide told us that for her courage, Flora soon found herself in the Tower of London. I imagined her being handed over to the keeper with full knowledge that many who entered the grim prison faced beheading at the whim of the monarch. Aiding and abetting a pretender to the crown of England was most certainly treasonous and yet she was considered a heroine by many and visited by the famous men of the day, including Dr. Johnson. As I stood beside Colin, looking over the water, I wondered how she kept her spirits so far away from this lovely spot.

Next stop was Inverness, the 'Capital of the Highlands' and the site of the Battle of Culloden where the English forces defeated Flora's prince and his men in April 1746. They say you can feel the pain of that massacre there, to this day.

Later that afternoon we headed for the beautiful Grant Arms Hotel at Grantown-on-Spey stopping along the way to photograph some of the crofters' small homes. Some excellent single malt whisky not only warmed us but helped dispel the lingering sadness with which we had left Culloden.

The next morning after some excellent fine ground Scottish oatmeal and thick cut bacon with eggs, tea and toast, our tour took us to the coast of the North Sea where we watched the fishermen bring in their catch. We then headed north to Forres, a very old town with healthy invigorating air. King Duncan held court at Forres and it was on the way there that Macbeth and Banquo met the witches on the 'blasted heath'. The weather was so glorious that it was difficult to picture the eerie mists surrounding the hags and their boiling cauldron.

Following the coast road we reached Elgin, a market

town in the rich lands of Moray. Its royal castle stood from the twelfth to the fifteenth centuries and was occupied in 1296 by Edward I of England. The town's greatest glory is its cathedral, possibly the most beautiful of all the Scottish cathedrals, completed by the end of the thirteenth century.

After greeting us back on the bus the next morning, our tour guide explained that we were about to see, Fochabers, on the River Spey, an exceptional example of Georgian town planning. Unfortunately the A96 bisects the village square with its beautiful Georgian church. It did seem a shame that current planners did not see fit to respect the urban heritage here.

Baxters, the well known food processors and soup makers (cockaleekie soup is one of the traditional Scottish soups they make) is located in Fochabers' western twin village of Mosstodloch. Baxters is still family-run and has been operating since 1868.

The Grampian region in which we were travelling has sixty of Scotland's malt whisky distilleries out of a total of 110.We would be visiting the Glenfiddich distillery but first our guide educated us about whisky. We all hoped there'd be an opportunity for sampling.

Whisky is the spelling used in Scotland and for Canadian rye whisky. Whiskey is the spelling in Ireland as well as the US. We learned that the word Scotch is seldom used in Scotland. The best whisky is single malt which means it must be the product of only one distillery, it must be made only from barley and it must be made in Scotland. If it is sold as Scotch whisky, by law it must be at least three years old.

On through Strathspey, we stopped at Dufftown to have a guided tour through the Glenfiddich distillery. Glenfiddich means Valley of the Deer in Gaelic. William Grant founded the company in 1886. He and his nine children built the plant with their bare hands, producing the first whisky on Christmas Day 1887. We were interested to discover that the great washbacks used in the fermentation process are made from Douglas fir, a tree well known in British Columbia. There was an opportunity to sample this excellent whisky and also to buy a bottle to take home with us. We looked forward to sitting in front of the fire on a rainy day, nursing our whisky and toasting William Grant for his foresight and hard work.

In the morning we turned south to cross the Grampian Mountains. Passing through Colnabaichin and Strathdon we reached the Dee Valley at Bridge of Gairn and entered Ballater, home of the internationally well-known Highland Games, which have been drawing large audiences for over a hundred years. Eight miles on lies Crathie Church where Queen Victoria laid the foundation stone in 1895. The Royal Family attends services here when in residence at Balmoral. The grave of John Brown, Queen Victoria's personal retainer for many years lies in the churchyard.

In 1862 Prince Albert bought the beautiful Balmoral estate for £31,000 and had the existing castle rebuilt in the romantic style so loved by the Victorian readers of Sir Walter Scott's novels. Beautifully situated in a curve of the river Dee, since 1855 Balmoral has been the private holiday home of the Royal Family.

From here we turned due south to cross the Grampian Mountains where the road reaches the highest point of any road of this class in Britain, and on to Glenshee. There, the previously rugged highland scenery gives way to the greener pastures of Strathmore. The Spittal of Glenshee Hotel is a welcome sight to travellers over this road ('spittal' being a corruption of 'hospital', a shelter for travellers).

Journeying on south toward Perth, we first reached Scone, one of Scotland's most important historic places and once the ancient capital of the Kingdom of the Picts. The Stone of Destiny was brought to Scone, probably from Iona during the ninth century. Until 1296 the Kings of Scotland were crowned on this stone but it was then stolen by Edward I of England and not returned. A block of red sand stone measuring twenty-six by sixteen by ten inches, probably at one time a portable altar, it became part of the Coronation Chair in Westminster Abby.

We continued on to Braemar through Glenshee to Perth. We crossed the Forth Bridge, an elegant structure and one of the longest suspension bridges in the world. Just before we crossed the bridge we stopped at Loch

Leven, famous for its special breed of trout and one of Europe's most important wild fowl reserves. Mary Queen of Scots was imprisoned in Loch Leven Castle, on one of the loch's islands, escaping with the help of young Willy Douglas who locked everyone in the great hall and threw the keys in the loch. The keys were not found until three hundred years later.

Ten miles after crossing the bridge we reached the heart of Edinburgh, Scotland's largest city and its capital since 1437. Edinburgh stands on seven hills between the waters of the Firth of Forth and the 2,000 foot summit of the Pentlands. Walking along the cobbled Royal Mile, until 200 years ago little more than a cluster of houses, we were treated to a walk through history. The Canongate Tollbooth dates from the late 1500s and the Fifteenth Century John Knox House was built for Mary, Queen of Scots by the city's goldsmiths. Continuing along the Royal Mile, we visited the National Gallery which features portraits of all the Scottish monarchs from Fergus in 330 CE to James the VII in 1685. A guide took us through, sparing none of the gory details of their reigns.

Leaving Edinburgh, we travelled south towards the English border reaching Galasheils, a pleasant town associated with the woollen industry, with mills in existence since 1622. Close by is Abbotsford, the celebrated home of Sir Walter Scott who lived there from 1821 until his death in 1832. It was at Sir Walter Scott's insistence in 1817 that a warrant was issued to open the Crown Room of Edinburgh Castle and search for the

Regalia of Scotland, missing since the union with England in 1707. The Regalia were found lying at the bottom of a locked chest, hidden there 110 years before.

As in towns all over the British Isles at that time, rugby was the most popular sport, and it was here that the game of 'sevens' (seven men a side instead of fifteen) originated.

I was looking forward to Jedburgh where we would see the one time home of Mary Queen of Scots. She always seemed to me a terribly romantic figure. Famous visitors over the years included Bonnie Prince Charlie, Robert Burns, William Wordsworth and Sir Walter Scott. It was here that Mary Stuart learned that Lord Bothwell had been wounded and rode the 40 miles through the moors to visit him. The journey nearly killed her. Years later she is reported to have said "Would that I had died in Jedburgh."

At the visitor centre in Jedburgh, where her life is portrayed, one can see her death mask, supposedly taken from her decapitated body following her execution.

After travelling through the Northumberland National Park we crossed over the ruins of Hadrian's Wall, the northernmost limit of the Great Roman Empire, built so well nearly two thousand years ago that much remains today. It was erected to hold back the warring tribes from the north on instruction from Emperor Hadrian after he visited Britain in 122 CE. Castles and turrets were built along the entire length and regular army units were sent from the south to contain the local tribes.

We then crossed over the industrial plain of Durham to the city of Durham itself, one of Britain's most visually attractive cities with its Norman cathedral and castle perched above the town on a sandstone cliff, almost enclosed by the river Wear. The castle was begun in 1069. Our guide had instructed us to listen that evening for the curfew which has rung from the castle at 9 pm from 1069 to this day. The cathedral was begun as a shrine to St Cuthbert in 995 and the present building dates from 1093, being the finest Norman building in Europe today.

My father was born in Hartlepool in the County of Durham on 15th October 1884. As a little girl I remember my father talking about the great cathedral where he was a choir boy. I never thought then that I would see it. The castle and cathedral stand high on a hill above the lovely town.

Our next stop would be the walled city of York and another magnificent cathedral. We headed south along the old coach road from Scotland, the A1.and I wondered if my father's family ever travelled this road. Quite likely they did not. Most people in England up until the end of the 19th century seldom ventured far from home. Today, many of us have the luxury of both time and money.

The day seemed very long to us but I couldn't help

thinking it must have seemed infinitely longer in a coach along a bumpy road. We were glad when we finally reached the city of York.

York is a walled city whose history stretches back almost two thousand years. The minster, or cathedral is a glorious church built between 1220 and 1470, and it is a prime example of early English gothic architecture. Colin and I stood in awe surrounded by the greatest collection of thirteenth and fourteenth century stained glass in England. Our guide, an obviously proud parishioner, also pointed out the fifteenth century East Window, the largest in the world, the size of a football field. Often, in these stained glass masterpieces, if you look closely, you can find instances where the artisans put themselves in some of the images.

Although little now remains of the early York, the medieval city was all around us as we walked through the cobbled streets of the Shambles and Stonegate. In recent times excavators discovered the site of a Viking settlement, now carefully reconstructed to give a clear picture of life in Viking times in what was then called Jorvik, the derivation of today's York.

Heading back to London at the end of the trip, Colin and I looked forward to one last treat. We were going to see *Cats*. It was actually raining cats and dogs as we drove in a taxi to the theatre. Fortunately Colin carried his 'brolly' which he gallantly held over me as we dashed across the pavement from the cab into the theatre.

Chapter 5

Going Greek—Things Go Wrong

In the fall of 1987 Betty and Art asked Colin and I if we would like to visit some of the Mediterranean and the Greek Islands with them. Before long we were all poring over guidebooks that I borrowed from our local West Vancouver Memorial Library. Fodor's and Frommer's made it easy for us armchair travelers to picture ourselves sitting outside a picturesque taverna, sipping something other than retsina after a day of leisurely sight seeing.

The next Sunday, a typically wet spring day, after dinner and over coffee in front of a cozy fire, we looked at the calendar and decided on the first three weeks in May for our trip. Betty and Art had been to Europe on the 'grand tour'. That's the one where 'if it is Tuesday, it must be Belgium.' Nevertheless, they said they'd rely on me to make the arrangements and plan an itinerary which included Turkey as well as Greece. And, although Ted did most of the planning of the many trips he and I took over the years, I felt confident I could handle the tour guide role. Little did I know the challenges ahead of us as we drove to the airport in Vancouver.

In the weeks before we left, I kept a checklist at hand, reminding everyone about passports, vaccinations, traveler's cheques and enough foreign currency to tide us over the first day or so in Istanbul.

"Make sure you pack the essentials in your carry-on luggage," I reminded Betty. Although I had never lost my bags, I was not naïve enough to think it couldn't happen. In fact, Art lost his luggage on a railway platform in Mexico, so they didn't, as Betty said tartly, need reminding. I made sure Colin had all his prescriptions with him on the plane, as well as slippers and a good book to read during the long hours en route.

"Practice lifting your suitcases fully packed with everything you plan to take," I told them. "You never know when you might have to carry them yourself."

Of course, on a cruise, you can take as much as you like, but on this kind of trip it is best to take clothes that will wash and dry quickly and things you can dress up or down with a scarf or a nice, but not too valuable, piece of jewelry.

We were all in fine spirits as we flew from Vancouver to London, where we had a few hours layover before going on to Istanbul. The coast of Turkey was lovely and the people, eager to profit from tourism, were helpful. We visited the site of ancient Troy and saw what was purported to be the home of Mary, the mother of Jesus. I was fascinated by the Turkish people and, always asking permission, took many photographs of which I'm quite proud. I approach photography in the same way I do painting, taking time to compose a picture carefully.

Betty and Margaret in Istanbul with their Turkish driver

Betty, Colin and Art in Istanbul

Turkish girl at her loom

Margaret and Betty at Rhodes

Colin and Margaret at Troy

Margaret with an amphora for storing wine, honey or grain.

In less than a week we were on our way to Rhodes and Crete, looking forward to a restful few days on the island of Santorini.

Santorini was everything we had imagined back in front of the fire that Sunday afternoon at home. We stayed at a lovely hotel, with high ceilings and beautiful terraces, which seemed to have been built right into the cliff. That first evening, after a quiet dinner, we strolled the cobbled streets of Fira before turning in for the first really good sleep we'd had since leaving Vancouver. I remember feeling thankful that everything was turning out so well because Colin was not the natural born adventurer that Ted was, and Betty and Art had trusted me to make this a special trip for them.

A farmer in Santorini

Art and Margaret in Santorini

Colin before he got sick

On our last day on what is often called the Mediterranean's most beautiful island, we were ready to tackle Athens.

"Let's have dinner and then a relaxing evening. We can have an early bedtime and arrive rested in Athens," I suggest to the others.

"Let's hope there is not more eggplant on the menu," Art declared. His only complaint about the trip so far war was the ubiquitous eggplant of which the Greeks seem so fond. It was not a common vegetable in his youth and he never acquired the taste for moussaka.

Colin chose a café overlooking the water, where they served a buffet of salads and grilled meats.

"I don't like the look of the chicken," I whispered to Colin as we filled our plates. "Don't eat it!" I cautioned.

We noticed that most places seemed to display an array of grilled meat, obviously cooked earlier in the day, and I had wondered just how safe it was to eat. Although I come from a family where 'Waste not, want not!' was the rule, I never take a chance when serving or eating food I feel may have spoiled. I'm always especially careful about what I eat and drink when on trips and don't even trust bottled water when away. Colin was about to learn to follow my example. He ate the chicken that I suspected had been sitting out in the sun for too long.

"I'm sure it's fine," he replied. I noticed, though, that he didn't finish it – rare for him because he always had such a good appetite. At home he would try anything and I loved to cook for him.

The next morning, though, he was feeling very ill. I asked the front desk to send the house doctor, who, after examining him said to feed him rice. "I suggest that you fly to Athens immediately," he said. "Take him to a hospital as soon as you arrive."

I decided to go to a nearby 'pharmakio' before leaving Santorini, thinking perhaps the druggist could suggest something like Gravol to make Colin more comfortable until we got to Athens. I found the pharmacy, with its big green cross, open, thank heavens but I didn't have much luck making myself understood.

On the way back I met Betty and Art who could tell how upset I was. "Come and sit down and have coffee with us, Margaret" Art said. "We'll figure out something to do." In the café another customer, a young woman listened to me explaining Colin's symptoms, clutching my next to useless guide book.

"Excuse me," she said in perfect English, "Are you American?"

"No, Canadian," I replied, used to this question wherever we went.

The young woman took my arm and led me out into the street.

"I'm a nurse," she explained. "I couldn't help overhearing you. I hope you don't mind me making a suggestion. Your husband is in real danger of becoming dehydrated. I'm going to give you some pills that I always carry when I travel. They're an emetic and will make him throw up but that is what he must do to rid himself of the poison in his system. Make sure he takes these pills right away and then you must get him to the diagnostic hospital in Athens, where they will help him. Show this to the taxi driver when you arrive there," she concluded, handing me a slip of paper on which she wrote the name of the hospital and its address.

"I can't begin to thank you, "I told her. "I'm so grateful for your help."

She smiled. "I'm glad I overheard you," she said. "Now please, don't delay! And, look after yourself, when your husband is settled!"

As I hurried back to the hotel I couldn't help thinking how much easier this would have been travelling with Ted because he, being a pharmacist, would just stock us both up with pills to deal with whatever was the local version of Montezuma's revenge.

"You can't be fussy, Margaret, if you want to see the world," I could still hear him saying. "But that doesn't mean you shouldn't take precautions."

I was also mentally cursing myself for not getting some pills from our doctor in West Vancouver before I left. Greece and Turkey may have been the cradles of western civilization but they had a lot to learn about modern day hygiene. Bathrooms in restaurants were often primitive and I suspected that kitchens were often none too clean either.

I don't know how I got Colin up, made him take the emetic, which made him throw up, and then dressed and into a taxi. Betty and Art helped with bags and checked us out. By this time Colin was terribly weak and, although I didn't want to let on to him, I thought he might actually die before I got him to help.

 It was a short flight, thank heavens, because by the time we were settled in our hotel, he was very ill, shivering, with stomach cramps and a severe headache. I felt his pulse and it was racing. I suspected he had a high fever as well. To make matters worse, Colin didn't want to go to the hospital.

"Please, Margaret," he said, "I'm sure I'll be fine in a day or so. Can't you see if the hotel has a doctor on call?"

I asked the concierge if there was an English speaking doctor on call and was told it would take several hours before one would be available so I asked them to call a cab to take us to the hospital.

Betty and Art, meanwhile, had, at my urging, reluctantly gone off sightseeing.

"There's no point in you two waiting around," I assured them. "I've been here before and once Colin is feeling better, I'll enjoy the city, too."

As I helped Colin through the lobby to the taxi, I could feel people looking at us but, by this time, I couldn't have cared less!

"Please hurry," I begged the cab driver and showed him the slip of paper the young English woman had given me with the name of the hospital. "My husband is terribly ill."

In the cab I sat next to him, a plastic bag at the ready although he had, as the nurse predicted, thrown up everything he might have had in is stomach, including the chicken, back at the hotel in Santorini. The streets were narrow and bumpy and the day was unbearably hot.

"Please, God," I prayed, "let me get Colin to the hospital safely." I'd already lost one husband and I didn't want to lose a second. They say only the good die young. It was certainly true of Ted because there just wasn't a better man on the face of the earth. Colin was another really decent, kind hearted guy who would do anything to help someone in trouble.

When I saw the hospital, I was relieved. It was new and very clean and orderly inside. I waited in the emergency room with him and, after what seemed like hours, a doctor arrived and, in halting English explained that Colin would probably be fine in a few days. Soon Colin was settled in a ward, connected to an intravenous drip. His face was ashen but he seemed to know that everything would soon be all right. "We will keep your husband here for the time being, Madam. It is fortunate that you brought him in when you did."

I explained about meeting the English nurse in the café and about the emetic she had given me for Colin. He smiled and shaking my hand, suggested I might like to go up to the rooftop restaurant and have some tea before going returning to the hotel. I thanked him and did just that. I suddenly realized that I hadn't eaten anything all day.

"Well, Margaret," I said to myself, "You wanted to see Athens. Bet you never thought you see this side of it."

The restaurant was lovely, with huge plates of tomatoes and fresh fruit. I had some tea and a salad and then got back into a very crowded elevator to go down to see Colin. More and more people got on and I was pushed further and further back until, when I got to Colin's floor, the elevator was so crowded and because I couldn't make myself understood, I was unable to get out. Finding myself right back on the ground floor, I was determined not to be shoved to the back again and managed to get off on the next trip up.

There were three other patients in the ward with Colin. A nurse greeted me in English and told me that

Colin was comfortably settled. She told me she was from Montreal. There was also another English-speaking nurse from England.

I asked if Colin could have a private room but evidently none was available. As a result I soon got to know the other patients on the ward. One of them was a glamorous and excitable Greek actress who had been bitten by a cat in Rome and developed an ulcer on her leg. After a day or so I was acting as a volunteer on the ward, doing little errands, working on my needlepoint and bringing treats, flowers and magazines. I soon discovered that visitors could come and go as they liked. You could even stay all night if you wished.

At first, though, I had more immediate problems. Colin was very weak and I could see that he would soon be fast asleep now that he was in good hands. I had to get back to my hotel, contact the travel insurance people and arrange to rebook all the rest of our trip. It was now nearly five o'clock.

I kissed Colin good-bye, saying I'd be back the next day. Taking the same crowded elevator down again I stepped out onto the street, confident that I'd be able to hail a cab back to the hotel for a bath and some room service supper.

It was not so easy. Cab after cab passed me until finally I was in tears, tired, hot, dusty and alone in a city I hardly knew. "Why had we come?" I thought.

Just then a man approached me and asked, in English, if I was in trouble. I told him I was just trying to get a cab to take me back to our hotel.

"These cabs are all reserved, madam," he explained. "People have prearranged for them to go home from their offices." Then, he gallantly said I could have his cab when it arrived. I was so grateful and just barely kept in another flood of tears, this time of appreciation. I have never been a 'crier' even though I've had to deal with some tough challenges in my day, but my tears were almost about to overwhelm me on that day in Athens.

Travel insurance and American Express - don't leave home without them. However, don't expect that, if you need your travel insurance, it will be as easy as they say to access it. It took several days and several phone calls before I got things straightened out. One phone call cost me $25.00 which seemed a lot. When I signed the final hospital bill there were so many zeros I felt I was agreeing to pay millions.

After a day or so Colin was allowed a boiled egg and then gradually more solid food. He said to me, "You don't have to come every day Margaret." But of course I wanted to be with him, I assured him.

When Colin was finally discharged he was still very weak and we realized that our trip was over. I arranged for a flight back to Vancouver. He boarded our flight in a wheel chair and another one awaited us when we arrived home.

91

In the meantime, Betty and Art went on to the next part of the trip. I, on the other hand, saw Athens through windows – of the hotel, the hospital and taxi cabs.

Before we left Athens, I took Colin on one more cab ride and he saw Athens through windows, too. It looked good to both of us!

Chapter 6

Homes and Gardens

When we were first married I went to live in Colin's beautiful home in North Vancouver. I knew I no longer wanted to live in Florida and it was out of the question for him to move there anyway. I was glad to return to Canada where I would be near my sister Betty and her family. His family accepted me as one of their own right from the start and now that Betty has Alzheimer's I'm glad that I live near enough to visit her often.

When we decided to downsize to a condo it was partly because we thought we no longer wanted to do the amount of gardening that home-owning entailed. However, I should have known better. Being the daughter of a professional gardener, I can never live anywhere for long without planning improvements to the landscape. I suppose you might call me a compulsive gardener! Colin was another one.

Vancouver is a very beautiful city with so many shades of green in the spring and many flowering trees. There is just no place like it! The spring of 1990 was, even for Vancouver, especially lovely. As early as February crocuses and snowdrops were pushing their heads through the earth, camellias and Japanese flowering cherry trees were in bloom. Soon Colin and I had planted tubs of azaleas and rhododendrons on the patio of our condo and, this being beautiful Vancouver, before long the shrubs were too big for the location we chose for them. There was a narrow patch of land on one side of our unit and Colin and I decided to replant the azaleas and rhododendrons there. Visiting the local garden store we were soon lugging home compost, mushroom manure and more small flowering shrubs, and before long we had a lovely little garden along the side of our unit.

However, Colin also had a hernia which I hoped was not brought on by all the yard work. While he was in hospital for repairs, a committee from the strata council came to tell me we had to remove all the plants we had put in. One of our neighbours, it seems, had complained. Only one person out of the forty-two residents complained about the garden so I couldn't understand why that one complaint made it necessary to dig up the plants. Our property manager was sympathetic but adamant.

"I'm sorry, Mrs. Armatage," he told me on the phone. "I know you did a lot of work and also spent money on those plants but you'll have to take them out. Do you want me to send one of our landscapers over to do it?" I agreed. Colin certainly couldn't help and the sooner the job got done the better.

"Perhaps apartment living isn't our style," Colin suggested when I visited him that evening at the hospital. "Both of us enjoy gardening and we're good landscapers. Maybe we really do still want a house with a garden of our own."

So when Colin came out of hospital we went house hunting. But first, we sat down and discussed the features we wanted in our new home.

"I'd like a pool again," I said, "and a hot tub would be nice."

"There has to be room for my organ," Colin said.

"Three or four bedrooms?" I asked

"How many bathrooms?"

Soon we found a real estate agent we liked, Clare Hartree, telling her we wanted to be in West Vancouver and the house had to have a pool as well as be on one level.

During this time we had also been helping Colin's daughter Lynn and her husband Brett build a rockery at their place in Whistler. Clare knew where we were and phoned us to say "I have just the place for you! It's in the British Properties, all on one level with a gorgeous pool. It's not yet on the market. I've arranged to show it to you this afternoon."

Because the house was over 40 years old, Denny, our son-in-law, checked it out for us and could not find much wrong with it.

"You'll need a new roof," he said, "but everything else seems in good shape." What else was he looking for? A shake roof costs a fortune we soon discovered. The garden was a mess, but challenges are what make life interesting. I could probably count houses that I've owned, decorated and landscaped instead of sheep to put myself to sleep at night, I've lived in so many.

The only catch was the owner wanted cash. To raise the money we needed to sell the condo and also our place in Palm Desert. On top of that we had booked a South China Sea cruise, so we asked Clare to sell the apartment and we called an agent at the Chapparal Country Club to sell our place there.

When we arrived home from our trip we were concerned that Clare had not yet sold our condo.

"Don't worry," she assured us. "I'm confident I will sell it before long."

She knew we had to drive down to Palm Desert to finalize the sale of our property there.

"Just go ahead," she told me, "and don't worry.

So we headed south again. We were very fortunate

to sell the condo and our California property within four days.

Feeding the ducks in the garden of our Palm desert home

My sister Betty and her husband Art came down to help us pack up. It was sad to be leaving the desert but we planned to return, renting as many folks do. We sold most of our furniture with the desert house but shipped some things to Vancouver to be put in storage until we moved in February 1991. We had stored books in the garage and discovered when we opened the boxes before sending them north that termites had been busy literally eating up the glue and the pages. I was used to termites, as well as many other species of creepies and crawlies such as snakes, rats and alligators in Florida, once even an alligator on a neighbour's porch. But somehow I never expected to find them in the desert. Most of my books were destroyed.

I never turn a key in a door for the last time without pausing for a few minutes to hear the voices of friends and relatives who helped make the house a home. Many friends and family had visited us here. It was a way of life we were leaving as well, because having a place in California meant we could miss some of the endlessly rainy days in Vancouver. I hoped we were doing the right thing because there would be no going back. Our new house was pricey and no doubt there would be many hidden expenses when we finally moved in. Renting a place in Palm Springs for a much shorter time would be about all we could do.

Suddenly it was the end of February and time to move. It was quite a job. Like most people we had collected too many things. I have collections of dolls and ornaments, china and crystal, handicrafts and works of art, mementoes of my many travels. Also, Ted's mother gave me her beautiful silver tea service as her wedding present to us. She was so very good to me right from the day I met her. How could I part with such a treasure? Fortunately the new house was large enough to display many lovely things and I enjoy them every day.

Almost the day we moved in the roof, which we knew would need replacing, started to leak in the kitchen and when Colin went up into the attic he found a racoon's nest in the roof, little babies and all. I guess we scared them out and I can still see the mother leading them one by one over the fence down near the creek that runs at the back of our property. Racoons are something of a law unto themselves in this area, often coming right into houses looking for a change in diet. They are amusing to watch but can also be aggressive, especially the males. I discourage them because of the fish in my pond.

Once the new shake roof replaced the old one, there were no more leaks. Then we built a small addition to the back of the house to house the pool equipment, a hot tub and also four comfortable sitting areas. There's no doubt that pools take a lot of work but I enjoy mine so much and feel it is well worth the trouble and expense of the upkeep. I soak in my hot tub nearly every morning and swim in the pool every day from the first warm days in late spring until the fall.

A major house cleaning was necessary before we could feel comfortable. You expect to do some cleaning when you move to a new old house but this house was dirty. The stove was filthy and the kitchen drawers obviously hadn't ever been cleaned. It was disappointing since I always left my houses spotless. I learned early from both my parents that if you are lucky enough to own a house and have a garden you must look after things. "Hard work never harmed anyone," I can still hear my mother say. All in all, Colin and I were very busy.

Both Colin and I were book lovers so we had shelves put in the den to house what was left of mine and all Colin's favourites and also put another cupboard in the kitchen for my cookbooks. Basically, though, the house was in good shape for being almost forty years old.

The garden was another story. It had been much neglected. First we had a sprinkler system installed. Then Colin went to work on the fence that was falling down.

Colin was never happier than when he had a project. We'd both work in the morning, stop for a coffee break and then work again till lunch time. In the afternoon we'd take it easy, reading and swimming in the pool if the weather was good. In cooler weather Colin, a fine musician, spent many happy hours at the organ playing show tunes and the old standards of the forties and fifties. Although I still entertain friends here, the organ has been silent since Colin died and I'm always hoping that someone will come along and play it again.

I wanted a lily pond. My father, a professional landscaper, built lily ponds for customers until the Depression scaled down everyone's budget and I've wanted one in my garden ever since. The one Colin built for me even had a waterfall.

The next year Colin put a greenhouse on the south side of the house so we could winter our prize begonias and other plants which were not winter hardy. We belonged to the Fuchsia and Begonia Society for ten years and won many trophies for our begonias. Growing them is a lot of work but very rewarding and, for the two of us, it was a labour of love. You must start the begonias during the last part of February so it helps to have a small greenhouse.

Colin designed the garden house and supervised its construction. He loved it as much as I did. When I married him I gained a family; his children and grandchildren became mine as well. We loved entertaining them all in our new house, celebrating birthdays and holidays, swimming in the pool and relaxing in the hot tub.

Colin supervising the construction of the garden house

The hot tub house finished

Colin in the new hot tub with the grandchildren

Now, when I look out of any window in the house I can see the result of not only all our labour, but also the careful planning we did. There are many different flower beds, a rockery, so many rose bushes I've lost count, rhododendrons and azaleas, a small vegetable patch and raspberries. Gradually we grew more and more perennials so we wouldn't need to include so many bedding annuals, and before many years went by the garden had 'good bones' that reflected our labour.

At times people suggest that I should sell the house. I am, they remind me, in my mid eighties and should be sitting in my rocking chair looking out of the window of my apartment or seniors' complex. They are people who don't know me well. My friends know that this home gives me so much joy and holds so many memories for me. It is one of the things that keep me young. Of course now, with Colin gone, I have help with both the house and the garden. This past spring I had an unexpected windfall that meant I was able to have the house painted a deep sage green.

Owning a house comes at a cost and although I may look wealthy, I do have to watch my pennies. Still, I have my priorities and a good wardrobe of classic, timeless clothes, most bought years ago, so my expenses don't exceed my income.

Over the years I've had the help of Inger, a Finnish-Canadian lady who not only cleans the house every two weeks, but also, when she is finished that, insists on going out into the garden where she weeds, sweeps and even prunes from time to time. A top notch gardener herself, she is truly a godsend. I met this wonderful lady on the day we moved into the house. She was outside shaking rugs, working for a neighbour, Mrs. Bell-Irving, and we got talking about all the work there was to be done in the garden. I quite naturally thought she was the owner of the house until she told me she was the cleaning lady. Colin's daughter, Lynn, had phoned me from the new house the day before we moved in to say, "This house is filthy, Margaret! You'll have to get some help cleaning it up before you move in. The house is too big for the two of you to manage, anyway."

I asked Inger if she could fit me into her schedule and she agreed. Looking back, I think she might have liked the gardening challenge. Often, while I have been working on this book I'll look out my window and see her down on her knees, weeding one of the beds or moving one of the plants. And she says this is not work!

Finally work on the house was finished. We were tired but it was a healthy tiredness. The house was restored to its original beauty and the garden, at last, looked respectable. We were ready for a break — a trip to Alaska that we had booked on the Royal Viking Line when we were on the South China Sea trip the year before. I thought back to my last trip up the inside passage to Alaska when I was escaping from my unhappiness after marriage mistake number two, to Lou.

When I met Colin, a whole new life opened up. We were a good team!

Chapter 7

Return to China—South China Sea

In 1990 we were off again, this time to Hong Kong, where we would spend several days before boarding our ship for a South China Sea cruise. The city, fascinating as always, was much the same as the last time I had been there but I noticed many more high rises. In fact, there seem to be more high rises every day. We stayed in a very comfortable hotel, the Palace. We had a small den with a desk where I could write in my travel diary and also do some postcards for friends and family back home. A lovely added touch was the fresh orchids in our room.

We sailed from Hong Kong straight down to Bali, marking the crossing of the equator with the usual good show for the passengers. I still have a copy of the ceremony with King Neptune and his loyal 'court of the deep' on the Royal Viking Line. If the captain is in a good mood and can spare some of his ship's officers, they will take part in the fun as well.

Colin and I loved being on the ocean for almost five days. It was enough time to relax, recover from jet lag and get to know some of our fellow passengers.

Margaret writing in her travel diary

Crossing the Equator high jinx

Our first stop was Bali for two days, where our tour included a lovely hotel lunch at the Sheraton Nusa after which we were treated to a show with dancing girls in exotic costumes. They danced a Hindu legend and, under Bali's balmy skies, mimicked the monkeys who killed a giant to free Prince Rama's stolen bride. We were told that Indian priests brought this Ramayana epic with its heroic monkey general Hanuman, to the Indonesian archipelago nine centuries ago. In time, Bali embraced the Hindu faith, building a magnificent temple honouring local and imported gods who, according to the legend, guard the garden isle to this day. This dance drama of the triumphant monkey army, with its movements and staging, is a delight to visitors like us. We learned that it reflected the Balinese love of festivity and also the intense concern with religion at the core of their culture. Our guide told us that art, music and dancing, in fact nearly every artistic pursuit, has spiritual significance on this island. Testimony to this are Bali's many temples, from the tiny shrines set in shimmering paddy fields or tucked among the clutching roots of sacred Banyan trees, to giant temples with as many as a hundred towers. The Balinese believe the giant banyans harbour potent spirits. Grotesque, often ribald carvings ornament the temples. At these gay open air shrines, villagers gather for magnificent festivals in which artists in cookery and décor as well as musicians and dancers, play parts they have practised since childhood. I was told that mothers massage their children's hands every day until the children can bend their fingers backward, a necessary movement in Balinese dance.

Bali's abundant rice crops, five a year, are enough to feed all of her over two million people. Several different types of rice are grown, all of it, at that time, still planted in the paddies by hand.

Colin and I looked forward to our next stop, Surabaya, which like Bali, has many Hindu temples. We saw salt drying in pens on the shore; oxen and water buffalo ploughing their fields. It was very warm. Having experienced the heat of the tropics on cruises before, I kept cool by always wearing a hat and cotton clothes which have plenty of room to breathe. Still, we were glad to get back on board our air-conditioned ship, shower and dress for a before dinner gin and tonic.

The stop we found most interesting was Semarang,

on the island of Java. The Royal Viking had arranged for ten buses to take us to the ancient shrine of Borobudur. This was very interesting to me as Ted, my second husband who was a knowledgeable student of archaeology and architecture, always wanted to see it. "We'll see Semarang next, hon," he said one day, looking up from the National Geographic he was reading. It was a dream that was never fulfilled.

Margaret always wears a hat

Margaret and Colin climbing up the steps

I will never forget this fabulous sight. It had, only recently, been discovered in the jungle. Its name means 'shrine of the many Buddhas. Colin and I took our time, climbing higher and higher up terrace after terrace of stone, elaborate with carvings and spired domes. These stupas, also called dagabas, look like bells with small carvings of Buddha inside, turning the dharma wheel, the wheel of life. Buddha, the Enlightened One, often stressed he was not divine but the common man came to regard him as much a saviour as a sage, building shrines in his honour and carving his image.

Our next stop was Palembang on the island of Sumatra. The mayor of the city was there to greet us with dancing girls and martial arts experts. It suddenly felt as if we were in India as cattle wandered freely about the town and we saw oxen pulling carts on the streets. It was a perfect, quaint and unspoiled spot.

Cattle in Palembang

One face of Indonesia

Then we were once again crossing the equator, arriving at the great city of Singapore. A crossroads to many cultures, Chinese, Hindu, Japanese and Caucasian, Singapore has one of the largest harbours in the world. After visiting the Orchid Garden with its many exotic trees, we shopped on Orchard Road. I have a collection of dolls, souvenirs of my many travels, including one from Singapore.

Colin was looking forward to the Raffles Hotel, which is more of an institution than a hotel and is the home of the Singapore Sling. It was built towards the end of the nineteenth century by the three Sarkie brothers from Armenia. It is hard to imagine today but at that time Raffles was right on the shore. Now the hotel is quite a distance from the sea. Singapore, with its many tall buildings and lovely resorts and hotels, is also one of the cleanest cities in the world. The Raffles Hotel is the only place in the city that you can eat peanuts from their shells and drop the shells on the floor. Since we were there last, the hotel has been demolished and completely rebuilt.

Back aboard our floating hotel, we were bound for Thailand, where we would leave our cruise. Quite a few other passengers stayed at the same beautiful hotel as we did, right on the Chao Phraya River. It was fun just to watch the traffic go by. We learned that the water hyacinths, which we thought beautiful, were a curse to many tropical rivers and streams.

I love to swim, daily at home if the weather permits, in my own pool. I'm always pleased when I find a pool at the hotel where I'm staying. The one in Bangkok was beautiful, surrounded by lush tropical plants.

We had four full days to explore. I had visited Thailand before but this was Colin's first time and I wanted him to see all the wonderful sights. The Grand Palace, of course, was number one. It was like a fairy tale castle with its many beautiful gilded roofs on the temple buildings.

We also took trips on the Chao Phraya River to see the Temple of Dawn which soars above the river, to see the narrow long boats on the canals or klangs as they call them. On the floating market the Thais sell just about everything, including tempting fresh produce.

Neither Colin nor I ever expected to see elephants playing football but that was just what we did see in Thailand. They were well trained and Colin thought they were more fun to watch than the National Football League.

All too soon it was time to say goodbye to the Orient. We flew non stop from to Vancouver. We'd been gone three weeks and were looking forward to returning to our home in West Vancouver.

Thai monks in their saffron robes

The floating market

Elephant football

Chapter 8

North to Alaska

Cruising to Alaska is the dream of almost everyone in the Pacific Northwest. As well, visitors from all over the world, who have seen pictures of the magnificent scenery all the way up the coast from Vancouver, book these popular trips. I have been on several; some were better than others.

Soon after we finished the work on our new house we took a well-earned rest cruising to Alaska on the Royal Viking Line at the end of June. I had been there once before but it was the first time for Colin. During his single days, he told me, he would never have travelled alone even though, as a handsome bachelor, he would have had no shortage of companions. Women far outnumber men on cruise ships and some lines even employ unattached men whose chief job is to partner single women.

You can often find good bargains for cruises to Alaska if you are willing to go on the first one of the season, the setting-in-place cruise, generally in May. That is when ships that have been on the Mexico and Caribbean circuits throughout the winter sail up to Vancouver via the Panama Canal. By booking so far in advance we received an economical package, two for one for a twelve day trip.

Colin's daughter, Lynn, and her husband, Brett, took us to the ship early so we could take their children, Laura and Rob, on board to see an ocean liner. They had fun exploring the lovely ship with us.

Lynn, Brett, Laura and Rob seeing Colin and Margaret off to Alaska

"Keep walking and don't ask questions," we told them so they wouldn't attract the attention of the crew. "Look like you belong here." We assumed we were not supposed to have visitors on board.

We checked the seating plan and discovered we were at the Captain's table, quite an honour. It is always fun sitting with the captain, the only problem being that ship protocol determines that you should not leave the table after a meal until he does. However, our captain, Jan Fjeld Hansen was a very interesting and entertaining Norwegian with a good sense of humour who enjoyed his after dinner drink. Having sailed the Alaska route many times he was very knowledgeable. We had no trouble remaining at the table with him.

He explained that Alaska has one hundred thousand

glaciers, in a total area of 586,000 square miles. The cruise literature explained that while many are nestled in mountain valleys, one of the most breathtaking glaciers is located in Prince William Sound, sixty miles southeast of Anchorage. Here the Columbia Glacier sparkles in the northern sun, a forty-one mile long wall of ice towering three hundred feet high. Chunks of ice 'calve off' periodically, making a sharp cracking sound before tumbling into the sea with a roar. We could look forward to seeing the Juneau Ice Field with thirteen spectacular glaciers including the College Glaciers. We were not disappointed because, when we reached the first ice fields, Captain Hansen invited us up on the bridge for a spectacular view.

Colin, in June 1991, bundled up to view the glaciers wearing his Scottish tam

After watching seals on the ice floes he said, "I'll bet you haven't seen ice worms." Of course we thought he was joking. Ice worms? They are not a joke although you will see 'ice worms', pictures of strands

Margaret, in 2004, viewing the glaciers

of spaghetti, on post cards in the tourist shops. Like ice fleas, they do in fact exist. They are relatives of common earth worms that wriggle through partially thawed ice to lay their eggs in water.

After Glacier Bay we went north west past Valdez and Whittier to Seward. With a population of about three thousand, Seward is called the playground of Alaska. It is located at the head of Resurrection Bay on the Kenai Peninsula in south central Alaska. You can drive to Anchorage; it's 127 miles via the Seward Scenic Byway. Seward is also connected to the state's metropolitan centre by rail. It was named Seward after William H. Seward who was responsible for negotiating the purchase of Alaska for $7,200,000, about two cents an acre, from Czar Alexander II in 1867. It was considered by most to be 'Seward's Folly'; the purchase was obviously no folly.

A good guide book can make travelling much more informed and entertaining. Whenever I travelled with Ted, he always did homework for both of us. Now I try to read as much as I can, starting as soon as I book my trip. A very useful guide to cruising Alaska is the third edition of *Alaska, the Cruise Lover's Guide* by Paul and Audrey Grescoe. Reading this before you go will mean you won't miss any of the sights and you will understand both the ecology and history of this fascinating state.

The Royal Viking Line issues an information update every morning. This includes the daily programmes, all the entertainment in the lounges, information about some of the crew members and entertainers as well as the world news of the day. It will also list shore excursions with information about the history and geography of the areas you will be seeing. Meal and snack times are listed with hours for each of the dining room and bars. They even include the recipe for *The Drink of the Day*. Here is the one for June 24, 1991:

Celtic Surprise

Teachers whiskey, Irish Mist, a dash of grenadine, pineapple and orange juices

Blended and served in a beer glass

Garnished with a slice of orange and lemon and a cherry

I stayed with my Scotch.

You are also informed about the dress codes for the evening meals and events. I love to dress up and am still wearing the evening dresses I have owned for many years.

People sometimes talk about the massive amounts of food served on the cruise ships and while this is the case, you can order 'fitness' or lean cuisine if you don't trust yourself to eat moderately. Most of the time I don't have any trouble resisting foods which I know would put on the pounds. Of course, we all spurge a few times. This is a vacation after all and they do serve baked Alaska on the Alaska cruises.

If you want to know where you are there are always large scale maps posted. You can be busy every minute of the day if you wish or you can opt for rest and relaxation and just enjoy the scenery.

Just be sure, though, that you have all your documentation in order. Since the terrible events of 911 in New York, the US officials in Vancouver are very careful about whom they allow on cruises. People forget that, even though the cruises originate in Vancouver, Canada, they will be sailing into to US waters when entering Alaska. Unfortunate travellers have discovered that while they may pass through Canadian immigration officials fairly easily when flying into Vancouver, a short drive later to the cruise ship terminals they will then face US immigration. If you are turned away at that time because of missing papers, you will not only miss your cruise but you will also lose your expensive fare. The cruise ship lines will not refund your money if you miss your cruise.

My third Alaska cruise was a difficult one. Colin was dying. We had been married almost fourteen good years. We both knew he would probably not see the next spring although he did, in fact, live until the following April. His doctor suggested taking him on a cruise although I wondered how he would manage. He had recently suffered a stroke and was having some difficulty walking.

He was a good sport, though, and the crew were most helpful. Some highlights of that trip were the Mendenhall

Glacier and a trip on the narrow gauge Scenic Railway of the World to the top of Whitepass and back, past the cataracts of Bridal Veil Falls.

Margaret and Colin, at the Captain's table, celebrating their 9th wedding anniversary

Soon after Colin died I took my sister Betty on a trip to Alaska that served to confirm my fears that there was something seriously wrong with her. I had been planning to go to England to stay with friends when Betty called to tell me that her trip to Alaska had been cancelled. Her friend, Marie, with whom she was going, was on a waiting list for cataract surgery. Her doctor's office called that morning to say she was next on the list. I could tell how disappointed Betty was from the tone of her voice. I changed my plans for England and went with Betty instead.

It was early September and the weather, slightly overcast, gave a hint that the rainy season on the coast might be our travel companion.

Cruise lines prefer you to lock all your valuables in the ship's safe once you are on board but Betty couldn't remember the combination to unlock her make-up and jewellery case. When we finally got the case open she stubbornly refused to put her precious things in the safe.

Then, that first night she took too many sleeping pills. The trip was a nightmare and I soon regretted going, although perhaps it was just as well that I did go. Being with Betty twenty-four hours a day made me realize that she was ill. She has become progressively worse since then and now is in residential care.

Late this past summer my friend Roy invited me to go on still another Alaskan cruise. This time we sailed for fourteen days on the elegant Island Princess. We were included in the special social events reserved for passengers in the 'Captain's Circle' because I had accumulated enough days at sea on this line to qualify. The ship was beautifully appointed, our stateroom very comfortable with stainless steel fixtures in the bathroom, the food and service excellent. We didn't take any of the ashore trips but chose instead to relax on board. It was wonderful. There was one thing that disturbed me, though. I felt that the glaciers had receded. Back home again I compared my photos of them taken on my earlier trips with the ones I took in September. They had definitely receded.

Margaret and Roy in the Captain's Circle

Glaciers then and now

Chapter 9

At Home and Abroad in Portugal

Colin and I were well on our way to being world travellers who did not know our own backyard very well. Although I had grown up in New Westminster, after I married my first husband, Jack, I really never had the opportunity to explore BC.

"Why don't we do some island hopping?" I suggested to Colin one morning over breakfast coffee. In those days we often had guests from far off places, frequently people I originally met when Ted and I travelled. Also, Ted knew people from all over, partly because of his work with Rotary International and partly through his profession as a pharmacist. As I mentioned earlier, Expo 86 brought many visitors and during those few months we seldom left the city. There was so much to see right here.

Once Expo was over I began to give some thought to getting to know some of the islands between Vancouver and Vancouver Island. Colin's stepson, Denny, had taken us for cruises around the Gulf Islands on his yacht. Another time he took us from Pender Harbour up to Princess Louisa Inlet and Chatterbox Falls.

Many of the islands are easily accessible, some as day trips, and it would be fun to take visitors on a ferry ride to view the spectacular coastal scenery.

"I'd like to tour the Gulf Islands," I continued, "just to be familiar with the scenic spots, good walks and places to stay and eat."

"You should write a travel book, Margaret," Colin replied. "You're so good at finding the best places and you keep good notes."

It's true, I thought. Who knows, maybe someday I will write a book. Now, when I slip into my housecoat for an early bed, I enjoy reliving the good times I had with Ted and Colin, travelling the world. Those notes, plus the maps, brochures and photographs I've saved from my travels seem to wake up memories of people I've met and places I visited.

Back in the late 1980s you could arrive at the Tsawwassen ferry terminal, about a forty-five minute drive from downtown Vancouver, and be confident of a place on the next ferry to Vancouver Island or any of the beautiful islands in the Gulf of Georgia. We had no reservations for bed and breakfast accommodations either. Much of the world has discovered beautiful British Columbia since then and reservations are now a must.

The fall air was clear and crisp the morning we left for Salt Spring Island, Pender and Mayne Islands. We had made reservations to stay at the world class resort, Hastings House, overlooking Ganges Harbour, but decided to trust our luck to find places to stay on the other islands. We would end up on Vancouver Island, taking the ferry back to the mainland.

Hastings House is really an estate with accommodations in the main house as well as several other sites on the grounds. The cuisine is world class with produce grown on the estate. What I like best about this wonderful place is the lovely old fashioned garden.

In the fall we made our usual trek down to Palm Desert, this time renting a condo, to escape the 'monsoons', returning north in time for Christmas. Back in West Vancouver we learned that the Seymour Golf Club was planning a golf trip to Portugal. We also found that we could take the trip and not play golf, so we asked Betty and Art who were not golfers if they wanted to go with us and they said they would love to.

This time we flew to Rotterdam, then on to Lisbon. From the airport to our hotel on the beach was a much longer trip than we had expected from our tourist brochures. We discovered the taxi driver was a tourist, too. Needless to say, we did not take the most direct route. The hotel, when we found it, was right on the golf course and there was an inviting swimming pool. After our long journey with many hours sitting in close quarters on planes, I couldn't wait to get into my suit and head down for a refreshing dip.

The Algarve has 3,000 hours of sunshine a year, making it an attractive spot for tourists like us, not so blessed at home. In the winter months, however, it does not attract the hordes of Europeans who flood its beaches, resorts and restaurants in the summer. It was relatively quiet.

The next morning, when I came back from an early morning swim, Colin was seated on the balcony enjoying coffee and reading from our trusty guidebook.

Our wind-swept beach

"It says here," he told me, "far from the influence of much of Europe, Portugal directed its attention seaward. In the early fifteenth century Prince Henry the Navigator launched an age of discovery when he established a school of navigation on a promontory near Sagres. Rounding Cabo de São Vicente sailors and merchants, lured by adventure and riches, set out on a course around Africa bound for new worlds."

"I hope we'll be able to see some of the old fishing villages," he continued.

"Good idea, "I agreed, "Just give me a day or two to relax and recharge my batteries." A day or so later we were up early heading down the coast to see Tavira with its brightly coloured 'lanchas', small wooden fishing boats, bringing in the catch of the day.

From Tavira we drove to the Chapel of São Laurenço near Almansil. Here we saw Portuguese artistry and craftsmanship at its best. The walls and ceilings are covered in blue and white glazed tiles called azulejos, depicting the life and martyrdom of St Lawrence. I wondered if this was the same St. Lawrence for whom one of our great rivers in Canada is named.

"Look at all the chimney pots!" Colin said as we drove through one of the fishing villages. They were all different shapes and sizes. Something that has impressed me time and time again when visiting Europe is the respect ones sees for old houses and other buildings. I think that in Vancouver we are far too quick to tear down old places instead of refurbishing them. It seems very strange that nowadays new houses that look old are being constructed, often on the very place where an old house has been levelled.

Most days Colin and I played golf on some very interesting golf courses while Betty and Art enjoyed the beach.

I am what you might call a thinking golfer. When I first started playing on our homemade golf course in Kamloops there were some challenging shots. There was even one hole where you had to shoot from the tee over a highway and railroad tracks. It was necessary to plan your strategy and I had some good teachers in those days. Colin was not a golfer when I met him but when he saw how enthusiastic I was about the game he was eager to learn and soon became quite good. Not only was he a good sport but he learned to play a 'brain' game too. I must admit to a competitive streak so that when I played well on our last day and won a trophy, it felt good.

Margaret with her golf trophy

Colin in Lisbon

All too soon we headed back to Lisbon, leaving just enough time for a tour of this lovely city Lisbon sits on a series of hills above the Tagus River, while walkways, shaded by jacaranda blossoms, wind through city neighbourhoods. I loved the tree-lined boulevards and the simple elegance of the city's main square, the Praça de Comércio, with its classical buildings and baroque arch. A feature of so many charming old European cities is a main square like this one, where people gather to meet friends, share a meal and a glass of wine or simply to 'people watch' as we were doing.

126

"Life seems to move at a more leisurely pace in Europe," I remarked while enjoying ice cream at a sidewalk café.

"Unless you happen to be behind the wheel of a car!" Colin joked.

On our last day in Lisbon we drove out to Sintra. It's a paradise in Lisbon's back yard. Sintra is surrounded by a lush forest of pine and oak. A winding road leads to the Palacio Nacional da Pena which has specimens of trees and flowers originally native to parts of the former Portuguese empire. A lighthouse at Sintra shines right across to Africa.

"Did you know," Colin informed us from our Fodor's, "that in the 1400s the Pope divided the world in half, designating one half to Spain and the other to Portugal?"

As a testament of the wealth of the Portuguese empire, the ornate Monastery of Jeronimos in Belem, which is now in a Lisbon suburb, was commissioned by Manuel I to honour Vasco da Gama's discovery of a sea route to India. At the site of da Gama's departure, the Monument to the Discoveries was dedicated in 1960. We all remembered learning about explorers like Vasco da Gama when we were in grade school. All those lands in the new and old worlds seemed so far away in those days. I always thought, though, that I would find a way to see them when I grew up.

"How would you like to see a bull fight?" Colin asked us near the end of our stay.

"Not much," was my first response. I hate any kind of cruelty to animals.

However Colin assured me that in Portugal the matadors do not kill the bulls, so in the end I agreed. Knowing the fight would not end in bloodshed, I found the whole thing quite funny. What was funnier was the fact that the Canadian flag, for some reason being flown at the ring, was upside down. I now have a healthy respect for bulls and matadors.

One bull fight was enough, though.

Chapter 10

Maritime New England Cruise

Our new house on Taylor Way in the British Properties was just a few blocks from Park Royal, one of Western Canada's most successful shopping centres. Wooward's Department Store was probably the most popular store in the mall. Few people know that Charlie Woodward, the store's founder, got his start on Manitoulin Island before coming out to BC in the 1880s. Almost one hundred years later his heirs succeeded in running his department store empire into the ground and one of the first parts of the business to go was the well known 'food floor'. As a business woman myself, I'm well aware that owning your own business is hard work and takes a dedication to excellence. Charlie Woodward knew that too. It was just too bad that his children and grandchildren didn't understand that.

Woodward's was 'our store' because, like most West Vancouver residents, Colin and I shopped for groceries there. Woodward's had the best meats and produce as well as many specialty items you couldn't find anywhere else. Often, also, after the friendly staff loaded our groceries into the car, we would head upstairs to the store restaurant for lunch or a cup of coffee and a piece of pie. I guess I shouldn't be surprised at the way the coffee places like Starbucks have sprung up all over the place, although I have a hard time understanding the willingness of so many people nowadays to spend $3.00 and more for specialty coffees. I can't bring myself to spend that much money for a cup of coffee and still miss Woodward's where the coffee was less than a dollar, the meals good and reasonably priced and the waitresses efficient and pleasant. You could also be sure of meeting friends either in the store or the restaurant.

One afternoon in September, 1994, we had just finished lunch and were walking back through the mall when we passed a travel agency with a sign in the window advertising a Canada-New England Cruise. Colin and I had cruised to Hawaii on our honeymoon, and later in the South Seas and the Caribbean. The idea of a Canada-New England cruise intrigued us so we stopped in to check it out. The ship was one of the Royal Princess Line, line, eight years old. There would be 200 passengers; just the right size, I think.

I had lived in New England when I moved all the way from Kamloops to Maine after I sold my motel and married Ted and, although I was glad to eventually find my way home to the West Coast after Ted died, I always thought I'd like to go back to New England and enjoy the wonderful fall colours one more time. Colin had never been to New York or New England so showing him the sights would be fun.

Like Ted, Colin never asked if we could afford a trip, and sometimes now I think maybe I should have been more careful with money. I have to be careful with my spending now and save for any trips I do take but, all in all, I don't regret any of the wonderful times I travelled with my two favourite men. My advice is to follow your dreams. Even if things don't work out you'll at least have a good story to tell!

Map of Maritime New England Cruise

"Look at that," Colin exclaimed from our hotel room in the Waldorf Astoria, forty stories up. He just couldn't stay away from the window.

"Those yellow cabs lined up down there look just like the toy cars I collected as a kid!"

There was so much to see and do in the city we were happy to find a quiet restaurant at the end of the day.

The Waldorf also served a very elegant afternoon tea, dainty sandwiches on fine china with real English tea, piping hot. It has been my experience in the US that very few restaurants know how to serve tea the way I was taught by my mother. First you warm the pot with boiling water, and then pour that water out, add real tea leaves and cover them with boiling water. Boiling water is important. You let the tea steep for five minutes, then your pour it. Milk in first, tea after. The Waldorf knew how to do it in those days.

Margaret in New York City

New York holds many memories for me. Ted and I often visited New York during our marriage, sometimes on our way to someplace else, often to visit his sister and her husband and to take in a play or a show. One of my favourite restaurants in

New York in those days was La Forchette. Ted and I dined there many times.

I first visited New York on my own back in the 1950s' when I met my friend Joe Heron there. He showed me all the sights and wined and dined me at the famous Twenty-One and Stork nightclubs. He knew the owner of the Stork Club. Joe would tip the maitre d' there, who always gave us a good table.

Joe was a nervous guy, always chewing his thumb. Joe, a travelling salesman, was one of my motel regulars in Kamloops. I never really knew the details of his family life back in his home in Oregon, but I think I did know that my romance with him was going nowhere if there were a wife and kids in the background. He was lonely and, like most men, wanted a good listener. I guess we just lived for the moment that week in New York that we spent together. Joe said it was great fun showing someone you were fond of the sights in the city. I felt that way now with Colin but there wasn't going to be enough time to show Colin everything I wanted him to see. In fact, had I known it, there wasn't much time left for Colin and me.

We did all the usual New York things; the Metropolitan Museum, the Statue of Liberty, Staten Island and Central Park. We also visited Rockefeller Center and the World Trade Center. When I saw those terrible images on my TV screen on September 11, 2001, I wondered if I would ever be able to think about one of my favourite cities in the world without reliving that terrible memory.

Margaret and Colin aboard the Royal Princess – I still wear that dress

After those few busy days we were glad to board our ship, the Royal Princess on 2nd October. It was a beautiful evening when we sailed out of New York, the outline of the tall buildings and the Statue of Liberty silhouetted against a deep blue sky. Colin raised his wine glass in a toast, "Here's to happiness, Sweetie!"

Our first stop was Newport, Rhode Island. A tour bus met our ship to take us to see many of the 19th Century mansions built by wealthy American financiers in the 1800s. Most of these were self-made men with socially ambitious wives. 'Nouveau riche', as they were labelled by old families like the Roosevelts and the Cabot-Lodges, sometimes these people did not always understand the thin line dividing good and bad taste. The Breakers, built for Cornelius Vanderbilt in 1895, resembles a sixteenth century northern Italian palace, grand if rather out of place in that setting. Another Vanderbilt, William K., built Marble House in 1892. It still has its original furnishings as well as a Chinese teahouse. Henry James and Edith Wharton both wrote about this society and there have been some excellent film adaptations of their novels, Wharton's *The Age of Innocence* and *The Buccaneers* and James' *Portrait of a Lady* show the behind the scenes heartbreak of single women without means who lived in that society. I supposed if I had lived back then I would have been one of them.

Our next berth was Boston's bustling harbour, like New York, a first time visit for Colin. I had been there often when I lived in the East and Colin remarked that I probably could have led the tour of the old town. We stopped first at Quincy Market, built in 1826 to alleviate the cramped Faneuil Hall Market, which consists of four buildings filled with international and specialty foods. Markets are great fun to visit in any major city anywhere in the world because, not only do you see the local produce and handicrafts, you also can observe the local people and their interaction with the merchants. The only disappointment is that you can't take food home to cook yourself. Fresh produce always makes me want to dig in and cook a meal. Markets also often offer good bargains in clothing and jewellery.

Following in the footsteps of the early Bostonians, we walked to Faneuil Hall, a gift to Boston from French merchant Peter Faneuil in 1742, which still serves its original purpose as a place for town meetings.

The oldest building in downtown Boston, owned by Paul Revere between 1770 and 1780, reminded us of the Longfellow poem about the start of the American Revolution which begins

Listen my children and you shall hear
Of the midnight ride of Paul Revere ...

We sat in the Old North Church, best known for its tower where Paul Revere flashed lanterns warning that the British troops were approaching. As a young boy Revere rang the bells there for the Sunday morning services.

We had a walk on the Boston Common, one of the oldest public parks in the United States. These fifty acres were central to all Boston and were originally used by freemen to graze their cattle. Adjacent to the Common is the oldest botanical garden in the US. It was actually designed in the mid 1800s. Its pond is famous for its swan boats.

Finally we drove around Copley Square, surrounded by Trinity Church and the Boston Public Library as well as the John Hancock Tower. We also saw the old State House, the seat of the colonial government from 1713 until the Revolution. John Hancock was one of the signers of the Declaration of Independence.

Later in the day we drove to Marblehead and Salem, a very picturesque drive along the shores of Cape Ann. We had lunch at Salem, an old New England town famous for its witch trials in the late 1600s. We wandered through the old graveyard where you can read the tragic history of this terrible time on the headstones of the hanged women. I took a picture of one stone which read "Ann Pudeator, hanged September 22, 1692". There is also a diorama of the hangings in the museum there. A macabre sight. Salem, like most of New England, still has many buildings dating back to the time of the first settlers in the area, one claiming to be America's oldest candy company.

Salem Witch Museum

I told Colin I was looking forward to our next stop, Bar Harbor, Maine. Ted and I visited there several times when his brother Bob retired and he and his wife Lavola moved to Bar Harbor from Connecticut.

Bar Harbor, a wealthy resort our guide explained, is the gateway to Acadia National Park which was established to preserve the natural beauty of the cliffs and coves of the area as well as the thirty-three thousand acre forest. The park occupies the lion's share of Mount Desert Island which was discovered by Samuel de Champlain in 1604.

Our tour took us to the top of Mount Cadillac. The barren peaks of the island could not be called mountains by someone who grew up within sight of British Columbia's coastal range, but the scenery is very beautiful just the same.

Margaret admiring a winterberry bush on Mount Cadillac

We looked forward to a promised lobster feed that night; lobsters cooked as only Maritimers know how to do them. We donned plastic bibs to tackle the crustaceans, swimming in lemon butter, served with chunks of French bread and fresh corn on the cob. We were all glad that finger bowls and towels appeared before we were served fresh apple pie. What a feast!

Maine became a state in 1820 but the northern border with Canada was still disputed. British and American troops raced to build forts, threatening war. The dispute was finally solved with formal negotiation. The Webster Ashburton Treaty of 1842 fixed the frontier where it is today. The story I heard when I lived in Maine was that Lord Ashburton wanted the border much further to the south, straight across the middle of the state, while Webster wanted the St. John River as the dividing line. They settled it over drinks and Lord Ashburton lost. They say Webster drank him under the table.

Back on board we sailed up the Bay of Fundy to St John. The rise and fall of the sea is quite dramatic. Tides in the Bay of Fundy are the highest in the world because of the bay's funnel shape. Twice a day one hundred billion tons of seawater flow into it and then out again. This astounding volume is equal to one day's flow of all the world's rivers! At Chignecto Bay in the east the water rises fifty-two feet above the low tide level. A whirlpool called Old Sow is sometimes visible off Deer Island on the approaches to St John. There is a great abundance of fish and marine life.

Buses waited for us at St. John, located on the south coast of the beautiful province of New Brunswick which links Nova Scotia with the rest of Canada. Together they were called Acadia by the French who first explored the area.

On June 24 1604 on the Feast of St. Jean Baptiste, Champlain sailed into the river that he subsequently named St John. The French found the local natives eager to trade, and visited the river mouth frequently. However, no permanent settlement was attempted until the entire region became British. St. John reminds one of an English city in appearance. The first settlers were British colonists from New England. Then, in 1783, after the American Revolution, another influx of colonists arrived. Fourteen hundred loyalists fled the new United States. Our guide explained that the real character of the old town was established at this time. We walked around and visited Trinity Church, rebuilt after the great fire. The church features a coat of arms, the mark of the old monarchy, rescued from the council chambers at Massachusetts Bay.

During the seventeenth century there was bitter fighting between the English and French colonists ending in an English victory. Then followed the forced removal of the French-speaking Acadians to Louisiana and along the Eastern Seaboard. I remember, as a school girl, reading Longfellow's poem, *Evangeline: a Tale of Acadie*, which tells the story of the expulsion in 1755 of three quarters of the French speaking Acadians by the British. Evangeline, a fictional character and her lover, were separated during the deportation. I read it over and over, always knowing the two would be reunited at the end but always not quite believing it. I was a romantic even then. The Acadian culture survives to this day in Louisiana and the Maritimes; 'Cajun' cooking, zaideco music and local folklore owe their roots to the Acadians expelled from their homes.

The next stop was Halifax. I was a pre-schooler when I first heard of Halifax. My stepmother had been a nurse there at the time of the great explosion on December 6, 1917 when a Belgian relief ship collided with a French munitions ship which blew a mile high. I've read recently that this was the world's largest man-made explosion before Hiroshima. 2.5 kilometres of the city's north end were obliterated. 1,600 people died and over 9,000 were injured. In the cold and stormy days that followed misery intensified. It was so horrendous that, after nursing the wounded for several months, our stepmother got aboard a train bound for Western Canada, trying to put distance between her and the horror she witnessed. I've often wondered since how it was she decided to stop in Invermere.

Perhaps the lovely valley and the pleasant little town seemed like a haven to her at last. However, she was not there for long before the Spanish influenza epidemic arrived and she was soon dealing with another kind of trouble. In fact, my mother, who died soon after I was born, was one of her patients.

One of the very appealing aspects of this particular cruise was the fact that we really did have time to explore, either on our own or on guided tours. In Halifax we took a taxi to visit my old friend Billie Horn who, with her daughter and husband, drove us around the city and took us for lunch at a local country club. It was nice to be with old friends.

Soon we left Halifax and set a course along the Nova Scotia coast to Cape Breton Island. Passing the Gaspé Peninsula, we entered the Gulf of St. Lawrence and then sailed into the river. On a short trip up the Saguenay River we spotted a pod of beluga whales, very white, following the ship.

Back on the St. Lawrence we headed for Québec City. It is quite a sight to see it from the river. The hotel Chateau Frontenac dominates the skyline. As a place of culture and beauty Québec has few rivals in the world.

Ted always did his homework before we travelled. Every evening for weeks before our departure he would read about the places we would be visiting. "It's half the fun of travelling," he often told me.

Now it was my turn to keep Colin informed. Québec City, I read, is the only walled city north of Mexico and to walk in the narrow streets of the old town is like stepping back in time 400 years.

Touring the city, we walked on the Plains of Abraham where the battle between the English and French took place. Marquis de Montcalm of the French fought the British General James Wolfe. Montcalm was surprised by General Wolfe who found a way up the cliffs. The battle lasted only twenty minutes, at the end of which both men were mortally wounded. I remember seeing a picture of the death of General Wolfe when I was in school. Of course, to those of us with English parents, Wolfe was a hero.

That afternoon we took the trip to the shrine of Ste.-Anne de Beaupré. More than a million people a year make the pilgrimage to this church, the shrine of the grandmother of Jesus. There has been a church on this site since 1658. Many people seem to be miraculously cured of their ills here. Do I believe in miracles? I would like to but it is hard to have that kind of faith, especially when both Ted and Colin died prematurely of cancer.

Later in the day we visited the beautiful Montmorency Falls.

Back on board our Princess ship we headed to Montreal, once Canada's largest city and our final destination. Again we took a tour of the city, first stopping at the Notre Dame Church, the oldest example of gothic revival architecture in Canada. Restored after extensive fire damage in the 1980s, the church was chosen by the Trudeau family for the funeral of former Prime Minister Pierre Elliott Trudeau. My notes tell me that this massive neo-gothic structure seats 5,000 people and opened in 1829. Its twin towers soar seventy feet into the air. The western tower holds one of North America's largest bells.

Old Montreal, like Québec City, is a charming place to spend a day, with its restaurants and ateliers. We also saw some lovely urban gardens.

Colin and I agreed this trip had been a good one.

Chapter 11

A New Year's Party to Remember

Everyone who travels has stories to tell about bad trips. Lost luggage, missed connections, uncomfortable lodgings, incompatible companions or becoming ill are just a few of the things that can go wrong when you are far from home.

In the fall of 1992 friends from Seattle phoned to ask if we'd like to join them on a New Year's cruise in the Caribbean. It sounded like fun and was quite reasonable so we said yes. At the last minute, however, they couldn't make it. We decided to go anyway.

We flew to Miami for an overnight hotel stay, where at breakfast the next morning, we met another couple, bound like us for the airport, to fly to Aruba where we would board our cruise ship. Donna and Walt Janghaene were from California.

Unfortunately, when we arrived at the airport no one knew anything about our flight. Perhaps things have changed now but back then major airline scheduled flights took precedence over charters like ours.

144

The airport was crowded and there was no place to sit and nothing to eat. The airport was also terribly hot and, after standing for several hours, I had an attack of tachycardia, a type of arrhythmia which causes me to feel faint. Fortunately Donna was a nurse. With a take charge manner she had me lie flat on the floor and got me some water. This did get the attention of the airport staff, who immediately brought both a wheelchair and some food. I guess I learned a lesson. Now I carry a few biscuits in my bag so that if I ever get stranded I've got something to tide me over.

We were there all day. It was 8 o'clock that night before we finally boarded the plane and midnight before the crew of the SS Ocean Breeze welcomed us aboard the ship with a midnight snack. I never enjoyed hot chocolate so much!

The next morning we were on our way to Cartagena, Columbia, a very old city also known as Cartagena de Indias. Between the 16th and 18th centuries, Cartagena was once part of the infamous Spanish Main. Pirates lay in wait hoping to plunder ships bound for Spain laden with treasure: gold, silver, precious stones and hardwoods from the New World. One of those privateers was Sir Francis Drake who sacked the city in 1580.

One can see the legacies of both the Spanish regime and of the Catholic Church everywhere in Latin America. In Cartagena we visited an old monastery with a gorgeous golden altar high on a hilltop, the Palace of the

Inquisition, the Castle of San Felipe with its creepy dungeons, and the undersea wall across Bocagrande.

Parisians and New Yorkers have their dogs. The Cartagenians have their sloths. A little girl came up to me with one and insisted I have my picture taken with her pet. Of course she expected that I would pay her for the privilege. I didn't really want to hold it but didn't like to refuse. It wasn't that bad. The little fellow lived up to the slothful reputation. He was soft, furry and sleepy. And the little girl had her dollar.

Margaret with new friends in Cartagena

Margaret holding an unusual pet in Cartagena

The next day we sailed through the Panama Canal and although I have sailed through the canal several times, I never tire of the sight. Although all ships go through the canal under their own power, little 'mules' or engines keep them in line through the locks. The first lock, Miraflores, is about a mile long, after which we found ourselves in Gatún Lake where dancers from Panama City came on board to entertain us.

Cuna Indians coming out to our ship in canoes and in snorkelling gear

Margaret and Colin ready for New Year's Eve

What with all the delays in Miami, I had almost forgotten that we would be celebrating New Year's Eve that evening. There was great fun that night, Latin music, dancing, a conga line to break the ice and get everyone moving, lovely decorations and excellent food as usual.

We headed the next morning for the San Blas de Cuna Islands in the Caribbean Sea a few miles off the north coast of Panama. These islands are the home of the Cuna, a traditional society of Native Americans. Most of these tropical islands are very small, many surrounded by coral reefs. The islands are part of Panama, but are primarily administered by the Cuna tribe.

The Cuna Indians, most in dugout canoes but some also in the water wearing snorkelling gear, came out to meet our ship. They took us in these sturdy boats to an island where we picnicked on the beach before sailing to some of the smaller islands nearby. It is funny how much better food tastes out-of-doors in a beautiful setting such as this; a white sandy beach, swaying palms and the azure blue sea as a backdrop.

The Indians were very quiet, just smiling and pointing to their crafts for sale. There were brightly coloured tropical birds, mainly canaries and parakeets, everywhere. Many were pets, perched on the natives' shoulders and on their heads.

I think I can truthfully say that I saw one of the strangest sights of all my travels on that day. The Cuna bury their dead in hammocks underground in graves which are sealed but not filled in. An open-sided structure with a thatched roof keeps the soil dry.

I bought a doll and some molas – designs on fabric made with brightly-coloured pieces of cloth.

Brightly-coloured designs on fabric done by the reverse appliqué technique

On the third day we arrived in the enchanting Dutch island of Curaçao where we toured the colonial town of Willemstad. We stopped at the old slave market, now selling fruit, and toured a peanut plantation. I loved stopping at an outdoor café for a cool drink in the late afternoon.

Flying back to Aruba, our tour ended but Colin and I stayed an extra few days at the beautiful Aruba Sonesta Hotel. The hotel owns a private island to which they take you by super-fast speedboat. The restaurant on the island overlooks a white sandy beach, part of which is a nude beach. We took a look but I didn't feel like being burned to a crisp and neither did Colin. We enjoyed the flamingos and the delicious lunch.

The hotel also has a casino but I have never been a gambler. I guess Colin and I both knew what it was like to work hard for money and gambling held no interest for him either. In my first book I told how, after our parents died, my brother Jack became addicted to gambling and sold all of our possessions to pay our debts. That cured me of ever wanting to take chances with money.

Heading home, we knew we had left paradise behind when bad weather diverted our plane through Chicago to San Jose, California and when we arrived home to find Vancouver in a snow storm. No cabs were available but coming up from California we sat next to a young man from North Vancouver. He had his truck parked at the airport and graciously gave us a ride home right to the door. He even carried our suitcases in for us.

Quite a New Year's party it was!

Margaret enjoying sunny Aruba while Vancouver has a snow storm

Chapter 12

Cruising the Mediterrean

We had been married for 13 years when Colin's doctor told us that he had an inoperable prostate tumor. I felt my life was about to come crashing down on me when we got the news about the scans. He had been having headaches which, unfortunately, meant the cancer had metastasized.

The immediate prognosis didn't look good and at first I relived my last year with Ted. While I watched Ted grow frail and thin, I tried to listen as he tried to help me plan the future without him. Ted was a down to earth sort of guy and although I don't know how many times he said, "I'm so sorry, Margaret. I thought we'd grow old together," he was determined that I would carry on without him financially and emotionally secure. Ted gave me more credit than I deserved. I married Lou and got involved with Dick before I met Colin. I couldn't bear to think of losing Colin, but at least I had learned something by this time and wouldn't make those same mistakes again.

We had to tell Colin's family, his daughter Lynn and

her husband Brett, but we tried to put on a brave front, letting them think there was every possibility that Colin would recover. At first it wasn't too hard to imagine or hope that he might really get better. Dr. Janz was giving him weekly hormone treatments and he received a course of radiation at the Cancer Clinic in Vancouver.

The family celebrated my birthday, as usual, with a party in Whistler. I've been extraordinarily lucky in being adopted by both Ted's and Colin's families. I'm never alone on those important days in the year like Christmas, Mother's Day and birthdays that can make older people on their own feel neglected. His family was very important to Colin and he said it made him very happy that I was outgoing and loved to entertain them. "The more the merrier, Margaret," he used to say.

Colin's 80th birthday party

Grandchildren Robbie and Jennifer share a birthday with Margaret in 1991

That year we celebrated American Thanksgiving as we

152

A pool party at Margaret and Colin's home — the more the merrier!

A birthday party for Colin's daughter Lynn

Rachel and her girls, Hillary and Erin, at Whistler

had for several years with our friend Rachel and her two girls up at Whistler. It didn't take me long to adopt the American Thanksgiving after I married Ted. In the States the celebration, much older than ours in Canada, is not a religious holiday. Early in the morning he and I would get comfy in front of the TV to watch Macy's parade in

New York. The day before, I usually prepared much of the dinner so I could sit back and enjoy the fun on the actual day. I'm a believer in slow cooking the turkey so, while we watched the parade, the house would fill up with the delicious smell of the turkey cooking in the oven. Sometimes we spent the weekend at the cottage but, wherever we were, family and friends would be invited for dinner. It was much the same at Whistler with Rachel and the girls. Of course, here in Canada, Thanksgiving is celebrated in October and there is no public holiday in November. Rachel kept the girls home from school and it was always a special day at her place too.

By Christmas and New Year's Colin seemed to be holding his own. I tried to follow his example and take one day at a time. We both knew you can neither relive yesterday nor live tomorrow. Every day we had together was precious and if he wasn't in pain we both agreed to make the most of each one.

I've said before I do not like the rainy winters here in Vancouver. That cold, driving rain just seems to go on forever. I have a painting just inside my front door of people walking under umbrellas in just such a driving rain. As far as I'm concerned, the picture is a romantic fantasy and that's why I love it! The reality of the rain here is that it does tend to get you down if it goes on for long. Of course, our beautiful gardens on the west coast thrive on the rainy weather. I always look forward to spring. Every day after January the first I'm outside looking for those first signs of the season; the snowdrops, the crocuses and the flowering cherry trees on the boulevard on my street.

In January that year, our friends Connie and Ken in England wrote to invite us over there. I had known them since my Florida days when we were introduced by a friend of mine in Sarasota.

We talked it over with Dr. Janz who said keeping Colin busy was the best thing to do. I suppose both Colin and I were in denial about what was happening to him. In going through our pictures for this book I can see that Colin was failing. We found a cruise that was leaving in the middle of May for the Mediterranean ending up in Dover. That made it perfect as Connie and Ken could meet us when we left the ship.

We had to fly to London first and then to Athens to board our ship, the Royal Princess. We had been on her a few years previously so it was like coming home. Greece was our first stop. We enjoyed our tour of Athens, Colin

Spring in Greece

especially, because he spent most of the last time we were there recovering in hospital from food poisoning.

We both loved the Island of Santorini, which was the island

155

where Colin became ill. "I never thought we'd be back here again, did you?" I asked him.

"No," he laughed. "To tell you the truth I never thought I'd want to come back!" In the spring the island is a mass of flowers, especially the beautiful red poppies that you see in many parts of Europe. In my mind these flowers always made me think of the poem, *In Flander's Fields by* our Canadian poet, John McCrae, but when you see them in such profusion on a Greek island they are very cheerful. I've read, though, that the farmers in France regard them as invasive weeds and hate them.

As we left the Strait of Messina we were informed that Mount Vesuvius might be putting on quite a show for us in a few hours. Our captain told us we were in no danger but I was just as glad to leave the area for Naples and then we were on to Rome.

I was surprised to read in our guide book that Italy is a young nation in an old land. The father of modern Italy was Giuseppe Garibaldi, for whom one of our BC mountains was named. What we know as Italy today was a group of city states, often throughout history, warring amongst themselves until they united under one flag in 1870. The Roman Empire spread its language and culture across Europe before succumbing to barbarian invasions. During the Renaissance, the city states and beautiful hill and coastal towns of Italy awoke from the sleep of the Dark Ages. Churches, well endowed by wealthy families since the reign of Emperor Constantine, became, along with those families, patrons of the arts. Architecture, painting, sculpture, literature and music flowered here as nowhere else in Europe. Today, Italians live with examples of this splendour, seeming to take for granted what millions of tourists pay even more millions of dollars to see.

After a brief stopover in Rome we were speeding by bus on the Autostrada heading for Florence. Italy is one place I'm happy to let someone else do the driving. Italians love speed and tear around corners on the narrowest of country roads. There's a lot of honking which I don't find reassuring.

In Florence we walked across the Ponte Vecchio to the Uffizi Gallery and the Academia. I wanted to show Colin one of my favourite paintings in the Uffizi, Caravaggio's Bacchus. I couldn't believe the line-up when we arrived there but, because we were with a tour, we by-passed the patient crowd. We also saw the Pitti Palace and the

A centurion in Rome   *Pisa of course!*

famous Boboli Gardens. Wherever I go, I always look for special gardens, loving to see the native plants and getting ideas for garden displays.

Of course we saw the leaning Tower of Pisa but we could not go up it, as Ted and I did in 1961, because they were trying to repair it. Evidently it was leaning just a bit too much this time! Back on board we sailed to Monaco where we toured the tiny principality made famous by Princess Grace. The city was as clean as a hound's tooth, as my father used to say. Everywhere you looked there were flowers in gardens and hanging baskets. There was also a cactus garden I found very interesting because I recognized many of the plants that grew in my garden in Palm Desert. Not being dressed formally, we had to give the casino a pass. I didn't mind because, as I mentioned earlier, I have never been a gambler except in affairs of the heart.

I was looking forward to a return to Barcelona. We took a day trip to the famous Royal Basilica of the Black Madonna in the town of Montserrat, where they also have an excellent boys' choir. Montserrat is in mountains which have, over time, eroded to look as if they have faces on them. There is also a Benedictine Monastery there where they make the famous liqueur. The bus trip up the narrow winding road, tighter than paper on the wall, if a vehicle came in the opposite direction, was frightening. Once again, as in Italy, I was glad we had not rented a car. "Leave the driving to someone else who knows the roads," was Ted's philosophy — one that Colin adopted also.

It was a Sunday and I could see that Colin was tired so we rested in the cool church and watched three weddings. When we entered, knowing that Colin was very tired, I saw at once that there was not an empty seat anywhere. However, two little girls noticed us and got up to offer their places. Colin and I were very grateful for the lovely manners of these girls. After the ceremonies the couples went upstairs and kissed the feet of the Black Madonna. There was also a steady stream of pilgrims all day.

We had a good lunch – a Spanish salad with some excellent wine while we waited for the return trip back down the mountain.

Gibraltar was next. It was a dull day. Colin had been looking forward to this stop as he had a friend that was stationed there during the war. He was not disappointed. We saw the apes, which are all named after the British royal family, with their baskets of fruit. We went to the

Colin and Margaret about to see Gibraltar

top of the island, took some pictures, went into the caves and worked our way back down to our ship. I was increasingly worried about Colin.

From Gibraltar we made our way to the top of Spain to the city of La Coruña, a very clean and lovely city overlooking the Atlantic. Later we took the tour to Santiago de Compostela, a legendary city on

159

two counts. We read that the belief that the tomb of the apostle, St. James, was discovered there is the most firmly accepted legend in the history of Spain. In other words, since the Middle Ages, this lovely city has prospered by hosting thousands of 'Camino' walkers who, at the end of their pilgrimages enter the Cathedral, kiss the feet of the statute of St. Iago and give him a hug for good measure. They also crowd the hotels and enjoy the city's well deserved reputation for good food. Moreover this so-called 'city of stone' is of such great beauty that it's imbued with a magical air.

Santiago de Compostela, Spain

In 1985 UNESCO declared the city of Santiago de Compostela a World Heritage Site in recognition of its universal appeal. The carvings on the cathedral are beautiful; in fact everywhere we looked there were wonderful carvings, especially on the façade of the University. Later, we enjoyed walking through the city's narrow streets.

The next day we were on our way to Dover, England. I was relieved because it was obvious that Colin needed to be at home.

Our wonderful friends Connie and Ken Chidwick

were at Dover to meet us. It was so good to see people we love on a perfect summer day. The green fields of England and the bright yellow of the mustard fields lined the highway as we drove to their place in Wickford, Essex. The ship had been very comfortable but it was good to be in a private home.

Connie and Ken had taken time off from their work to show us some of the country near their home and told us our first trip would be to 'Constable country'. And it really was just that. We felt we had stepped into the world of *The Hay Wain*, The *White Horse* and *Flatford Mill*.

Constable country

That afternoon we had lunch at a lovely tea house; thin sandwiches of w a t e r c r e s s , cucumber and deviled egg, followed by delicious scones with clotted cream and strawberry preserves and ginger cake. The tea was piping hot!

Our good friends, Connie and Ken

The flowers at that time in England were at their best especially the roses which were just in

161

bloom, many of them climbers on people's fences and trellises. The English certainly know how to grow roses.

The following day we were invited to Windsor to the lovely home of the Hudson's. They had coffee and fresh baked scones waiting for us. We were to stay for a Sunday barbecue, but first they took us for a ride on the Thames. It was so fortunate that the weather was perfect so the ride on the river was great with many swans, and the view of Windsor Castle. We had afternoon tea at a friend of Pam's who owned the Waterman Arms on the Thames. It was so good to be with folks who live in the country. The barbecue was just wonderful. It was different in a way from ours, as they had sausages, lamb chops and just so many different salads. It was just a wonderful day in the very pretty and private backyard. It was quite a drive back to Wickford but the days are quite long in the first part of June.

Colin was tired the next day so we took it easy and enjoyed Connie and Ken's backyard. We were both very fond of their golden Labrador retriever. "Maybe you should get another dog," Colin suggested, knowing that before coming back home to BC I always had dogs. My first was my dear little Fritzi when I owned the Mayfair Motel. They were all such good company. I felt that Colin knew I would soon be on my own again.

Another day we drove to Cambridge on the Cam River. We took one of the punts that the Cambridge boys in their straw boaters polled under the many bridges along the river. We finally came to the bridge I had painted from a picture a few years before. I never thought I would see the real thing. Colin recognized it first. "Look, Margaret," he said, "There's your bridge!" And so it was.

Margaret and Colin on the River Cam, 'the bridge' behind them

Margaret and Colin outside The Perfect Setting Tearoom

Afterward we drove around the campus to see the many colleges. I think there are over thirty. We went into King's College Chapel, begun in 1446 and walked through the gate of St John's College. The gardens of seven of the colleges run down to the Cam River and form together a parkland of great beauty; the famous so called 'backs'. We stopped in the town at a very old tea house, the Perfect Setting Tearoom. Just like the Brits, we were ready for a 'cuppa' with more dainty sandwiches and scones with clotted cream and jam. On the way back to Connie's, Colin complained he had a bad pain in the back of his neck and it didn't go away. He very seldom complained so I was glad that we were leaving for home the next afternoon. We had dinner that evening at the Barge Inn, a very old public house that served the traditional roast beef and Yorkshire pudding. One end was the pub and very noisy and the other quiet and sedate Connie and Ken drove us to Heathrow the next day.

At home again, it was summer and the garden, at last, was beginning to show all the hard work we had put into it. The rhododendrons and azaleas were in full bloom and our hanging baskets and pots with their fuchsias, geraniums and lobelia were showing promise of many blooms to come beside the swimming pool. Colin seemed better and I thought that getting away had done him some good. However, we had only been home about two weeks when, while he was clearing up the tulips, he came to the door in agony and said his back was killing him. I got him to bed and made him a light supper but he said he felt so tired he did not want anything to eat.

I went to bed, very worried about him. I took the phone of the hook because I didn't want him to be disturbed. Later that night, when he got out of bed he slipped to the floor. Luckily I heard him because he could neither walk nor speak. I called 911 and the firemen came before the ambulance crew. They all were very helpful and gentle with him. I phoned his daughter, Lynn and she and her husband Brett, both came straight to the hospital. The doctor said that Colin had had a stroke and that he probably wouldn't last the night. I stayed with him until Brett insisted on taking me home.

Colin surprised us all. He not only recovered after a

month the hospital, he came home determined to talk and walk. My wonderful friend Mary Rochford told me what to expect in the weeks to come. A nurse, she had cared for her father after a stroke. When Colin finally came home I took him to therapy three times a week. It was amazing that, by sheer determination, he did recover his speech and could walk again. Dr Janz said to take him on another trip, so we went to Alaska again. It was easier for me to take care of him on the ship because I didn't have any housework to do or meals to prepare. I was always glad that we had that last holiday together. He wanted to see Telegraph Cove again and he did from the ship.

We had one more fall and Christmas. Spring came, a very beautiful one, but Colin was in quite a bit of pain and needing more and more medication to control it. It was hard. I did not get much sleep. The doctor told me to keep him walking a little but he was in so much pain it seemed cruel. Near the end the home care people sent a man to help with his shower. At the end of March he went into palliative care. Colin was only there for a week when he passed away, April 5 1998 — the end of another beautiful marriage. The nurses in the palliative care unit were angels and I could not thank them enough. I was on my own again.

Colin Armatage
September 21,1914
to April 5, 1998

Chapter 13

After Colin

Colin and I loved it when friends from out of town paid us a visit. It often gave us the opportunity to repay the hospitality we received when we were travelling. Connie and Ken had been very good to us when we were in England and we looked forward to entertaining them in Vancouver. I met Connie and her first husband, Gavin, in Florida. Gavin was a bird watcher and he and Connie were visiting a mutual friend who knew about the lovely birds in my garden. At the time Connie had to return to England before Gavin so I invited him over for bird watching and breakfast on my patio. Connie, who now lives in Perth, has been a good friend since then.

When she and Ken came over from England shortly after Colin passed away, Connie said she heard in my voice when we talked on the phone the struggle I was having adjusting to Colin's death. She was sympathetic but practical when I told her I still had not collected Colin's ashes from the funeral home.

"I just can't seem to make up my mind about anything these days," I told her.

167

"Well, let's collect Colin and take him for a ride in your Cadillac up to Minter Gardens," she said. Their friends told them about the lovely gardens near the Fraser Valley town of Chilliwack, she explained.

"I know that you are grieving, Margaret, and no one can speed up that process, but it will help if you can get away from it all for a few hours." I knew it would do me good to see them.

"Bring your sister, Betty, as well," she added. I thought it was a nice idea but also hoped that Betty, who had been acting increasingly strange in the last year or so, would not be in one of her argumentative moods. She could become angry over trivial things and also seemed more forgetful at times. We didn't realize that Betty was showing the early signs of Alzheimer's. Nobody could disagree with Betty on anything because we knew this would provoke an unpleasant outburst. We were particularly careful when we were out in public places such as restaurants or theatres because Betty seemed oblivious to the other people around us. Betty's illness progressed steadily and she is now no longer able to live on her own. Of course I visit her and still take her out but I dread a scene.

It was a lovely spring day and I thought how much Colin would have enjoyed the trip. My friend at my service station in West Vancouver filled up the gas tank for me and checked the oil and the tires.

"She's all ready to go, Mrs. Armatage," he said, giving

a final polish to the windshield. I thanked him, thinking how dependent I had become on the men in my life to do those little things like filling the gas tank and checking the oil in the car. I thought then and there, that even if it did cost me a few pennies more, I'd always let someone else do these things for me. The attendants at the station are always so polite and obliging. Good service means good business in a place like West Vancouver, a community with a great many senior citizens, a lot of them women.

The gardens, conceived by master gardener Brian Minter, were glorious. Many of the flowering trees were in full bloom and there were tulips everywhere. It is a delightful drive about 60 miles from Vancouver along Highway 1. Although from the freeway you don't see much of the bedroom communities of Langley and Abbotsford in the Fraser Valley as you near Chilliwack itself you become aware of verdant farmland on both sides of the road. People still travel up here from the city in summer and fall to buy fresh fruit and vegetables from roadside stands. There is nothing like freshly picked Chilliwack corn! You can also pick your own strawberries and raspberries, buy many different varieties of apples and visit a hazelnut farm. Children love the corn maze that one farm family have created in their corn field.

Every gardener who listens to CBC radio knows Brian Minter. He is on the noon hour phone-in show with Mark Forsythe every second Thursday, as well as another local station on Saturday mornings, answering gardening questions on everything from landscaping to pest control. A small dark-haired man with a fast delivery, he makes you feel he is talking only to you as he suggests solutions to both common and unusual garden concerns.

Connie and Ken at Minter Gardens

I can't remember if we caught sight of Brian himself that day but we did have a delicious lunch in the dining room at the gardens before driving back home in the afternoon, just in time to miss the traffic jams into the city an hour or so later.

When we got back to my place Connie said, "I can see that this day out did you a world of good, Margaret. Come on. Let's get you away from here for a few days. Why don't we take the ferry over to Vancouver Island and visit Telegraph Cove again?" Colin and I had taken them to the north end of the island ten years ago and they were eager to return. They were fascinated by the rugged scenery and the history of the area.

I admit that I found it difficult without Colin. We enjoyed so many of the same things; music and dancing, gardening, travelling and meeting new people. I've mentioned that he was essentially a shy man but often

170

told me it was easy getting to know people when he was with me. I wouldn't exactly call myself an extrovert but having been in the motel business for several years I was used to meeting strangers and making them feel welcome. I find that being a good listener, which means really being interested in what people are saying, you can get along in almost any social setting.

We also enjoyed our home. We didn't go out that much when we were not travelling because we had everything we needed right where we were. However, with Colin gone, I found it difficult going out alone at all although I was fine at home. Even shopping or picking up dry cleaning seemed a chore. I was so used to doing things with Colin. Maybe I was just plain tired because nursing Colin in the last few months was exhausting. Now, when I volunteer once a week with the Eastern Star, folding dressings for cancer patients, I hope I'm helping to make things just a bit easier for not only the patients but also for caregivers. Of course, you are never prepared when a loved one dies, even if you know, as I did with both Ted and Colin, that there was little or no chance of recovery.

Connie and Ken came to stay with me the night before we set off for Vancouver Island. Telegraph Cove, on the northeast coast of Vancouver Island, is now a heritage site. Colin lived in Telegraph Cove back in 1935, in a house which had been towed from Beaver Cove on the east coast of the island. His tiny house was still there. The village, which was the telegraph station originally, had a cosy pub with a blazing fireplace in the round. The weather had turned damp and chilly and we were glad to warm ourselves in front of it and then relax over a very good meal.

We decided to stay the night but the pub owners were not keen to give us breakfast in the morning and there didn't seem to be anyplace else to eat. However, when I told them that I was Colin Armatage's wife and that he had recently passed away the couple said they remembered him well and that they'd be glad to give us a meal in the morning.

Crouter House, Colin's house at Telegraph Cove

I guess the community telegraph network was still working just fine because the next morning, while we were enjoying our scrambled eggs, bacon and toast plus mugs of steaming hot coffee, a few of the old timers came in to pay their respects. They all remembered Colin. Somehow it was comforting to talk

In the pub at Telegraph Cove

172

The history of Colin's house

with people who had known him. He had been there in the thirties, working in the mill where they made wooden boxes in which to ship salmon to Japan.

Later we headed back down the island to visit with friends, the McPhersons. I had known them for over sixty years. After a visit to Butchart Gardens in weather that had improved, we headed back to West Vancouver.

On the day before Connie and Ken left for England, my friend Arlene dropped by to meet them. I remember her saying, "Margaret is so lucky to have good friends like you!"

They had invited me to stay with them in England in the fall and Connie said, "Well why don't you come along with Margaret in the fall?"

I didn't say anything at the time and, after they left, I had plenty to occupy me in the garden. Digging up the spring bulbs, planting the annuals and hanging baskets, dividing up the perennials, pruning and weeding. Even with Inger, my wonderful Finnish helper, all my time was filled.

In the meantime, the Hollyburn Funeral Home,

which had handled Colin's funeral, sent a lady up every week to see how I was doing. I had my guardian angel it seemed. I mentioned to her that I wouldn't mind joining the lawn bowling club and she said she had been visiting Millie Newcombe, who was also recently widowed. Millie was active in the West Van Lawn Bowling Club and she was soon calling to arrange some lessons for me. It was just what I needed. It got me out of the house. It made some new friends and actually, this confirmed golfer found it was fun.

With the garden, lawn bowling and friends often dropping by for tea and some of my cucumber and cream cheese sandwiches I was busy, until before I knew it, it was time to get ready for my trip to England. I had actually forgotten about Connie's invitation to my friend Arlene. She had not and phoned to ask if the trip was still on and if she was still invited. She mentioned that she was thrilled to be invited but was having a hard time making ends meet. It had been a very long time since I had travelled anywhere on my own and I thought it might be a good idea to have a companion. Without really thinking much about it, I said I would pay her fare and asked her over to talk about the trip. We sat at the kitchen table while I also explained that, because Connie and Ken were both working full time, it would not really be fair to stay with them for the entire three weeks we would be in England. I asked "If I pay your air fare, could you afford a trip up to Scotland or Yorkshire?" She said she could manage that so Ken's sister-in-law arranged an itinerary to Yorkshire for us.

Lynn, my step daughter, drove us to the airport and when we picked Arlene up Lynn raised her eyebrows, silently asking "Did she leave anything at home?" Arlene had several heavy suitcases. If I'm flying anywhere I pack the bare essentials. My needlework and my books are more important to me than my wardrobe and I always manage to dress well and warmly, if necessary, without needing a fork lift to move my bags.

When we arrived at the airport and had checked, in Arlene took off for something to eat. I told her that we would be served a meal on the plane but she couldn't seem to sit still. After she disappeared, while we were waiting in the departure lounge, an airline staff member came up to me and asked if I was travelling alone. I replied "No, I'm travelling with a friend." She then said that they wanted to upgrade me to first class and, in the end, both Arlene and I moved from the cramped economy class to much pleasanter and roomier seats. Unfortunately once we were on our way, the alcohol was complimentary and Arlene took full advantage of this. She became quite loud and I began to wish I had left her back in Vancouver. I was relieved when she finally fell asleep. She was, however, noisy even when asleep. Her snoring kept me awake.

Ken met us at Heathrow and put Arlene and her luggage in the back seat. I could tell she was annoyed and thinking she should be sitting in the front with Ken. However I thought that Connie and Ken were, after all, my friends and I was also at least twenty years older than she was.

Connie and Ken had a very lovely home in Wickford, Essex. Downstairs are the kitchen, living and dining rooms and a bathroom. Upstairs there are three bedrooms, two bathrooms and a computer room. Their pretty guest room has twin beds, each with a cozy white duvet, and there are lovely white lace overlays on the pillows. Arlene and I were going to be very comfortable.

I liked to get up in the morning, come down to have breakfast with Connie and Ken before they went to their work as store detectives. Then I could load their dishwasher and do a bit of tidying up for them. Arlene, on the other hand, slept late and took her breakfast back to bed. Every day I worried about those white duvets, imagining coffee stains all over one of them.

Once up though, Arlene had to be on the move all the time. She loved to shop. What she chose to do was fine by me but I didn't want to shop or spend my time riding the local buses. I stayed at home, read my books and worked on my needlepoint. When she came home with a new coat and several other things, I couldn't help recalling that she had not been able to pay for her airline ticket. To be fair, I later discovered she was buying things from what the British call charity stores. They are like our Value Village or Sally Ann stores.

When we left for our stay in Yorkshire, Connie drove us to the station to catch a bus to London where we transferred to our tour bus. Riding a tour bus in England differs from being on a tour bus in the US or Canada in one way. In England you are assigned a seat which is yours for the entire tour, while in North America you can sit anywhere you like. The tour buses make pit stops along the way and generally there is food available, but it is usually quite expensive because the tourists are a captive group at the pit stops. Most people didn't buy food at these stops but Arlene always did.

I was delighted when we arrived at a lovely old hotel in Harrowgate, where we would stay. We would be taking side trips out of the city, as well as seeing much of the walled city of York. This was another shopping opportunity for Arlene. Once we arrived in York and were walking through the Shambles she was off again. In the afternoon she came running out of a pawnshop asking me to let her use my Master Card to buy a ruby ring she fancied. "It's only 100£," she said.

"That would be about $200 Canadian," I replied. "I'm sorry, Arlene, but I can't do it." For some reason she seemed to think that I had said I would let her use my credit card.

Every other day our tour took us into the Yorkshire countryside, into the Yorkshire Dales, where one sees sheep everywhere as well as lovely little streams and quaint old churches. One day we saw the place where the popular television series about a Yorkshire country vet, *All Creatures Great and Small*, was filmed. The Yorkshire countryside is very peaceful, the folks friendly and seemingly unhurried.

In the city we had a tour of Yorkminster, the beautiful church which hosts over two million visits a year. As they say, "Prayers have been offered for over 1,000 years!" Just the stained glass windows alone would take many days to see.

On our last day in York Arlene wanted to shop again but I told her, "I'm no shopper. Why don't we go to Betty's?" Betty's is the famous tea shop in York, a truly pampering experience. It's a very elegant restaurant where they serve lovely light meals and English teas with scones and clotted cream, scrumptious baked goods and of course, the very best piping hot English tea. While you are enjoying your meal a pianist plays show tunes and light classics on a grand piano. I don't think Arlene really appreciated Betty's. She was eager to go back to the shops so I said I'd meet her back at the hotel later in the afternoon.

While I was paying for our tea a charming couple behind me asked where I was from. When I said Canada, the usual question followed. "What part of Canada?" they wanted to know.

When I told them I was from West Vancouver they said they had lived there too.

"Are you enjoying York?" they inquired. They invited me to visit the botanical gardens with them and I agreed, saying that walking on garden paths would be much easier on the feet than walking on the pavement.

"We'd like to take you there," they offered. Soon I was sitting in their beautiful Rolls Royce about to enjoy, on that beautiful day, what was undoubtedly the highlight of my trip, the Harlow Carr Botanical Gardens.

In 1950 the Northern Horticultural Society leased 26 acres of woodland, pasture and arable land from the Harrogate Corporation in order to set up an experimental garden to test plants suitable for northern climates. I could feel my green thumbs itching as we walked through the ornamental plant trials area and followed some of the paths beside a meadow, a stream and woods. There are also peat terraces where shade plants are grown, an arboretum and a rock garden. The arboretum, which included many conifers as well as deciduous trees, was ablaze with rowan berries. I was very impressed with the limestone rock garden and the winter garden with its many viburnums and hellebores. A garden can be a very healing place. I knew I needed to return home to plan my own spring garden, just as Colin would have wanted me to do.

After a delightful and restorative time in the garden, my new friends treated me to an English tea in the garden restaurant and I did a little shopping myself. I purchased a lovely set of wind chimes that hang in my garden today.

They drove me back into the city, dropping me off at the hotel. I thanked them for their kindness and made sure they had my phone number.

"Be sure to call if you ever come back to the West Coast," I told them. "We have wonderful gardens including several lovely ones right in Vancouver."

Suddenly all I wanted to do was to go home, back to the garden that Colin and I had made together. That's where I would find him. Then the tears came.

Colin in the breakfast nook not long before he passed away

When Arlene and I returned to Connie and Ken's they had arranged a trip for us both into London with Ken's brother and sister in law. When we came back, Connie had a surprise for me. She had planned a party for my 80th birthday at a restaurant Colin and I had been to with them on our last trip. Eighty years is quite a landmark and of course the occasion was bittersweet because I couldn't help thinking how much better it would have been to celebrate with Colin. I was thankful, though, for good friends like Connie and Ken and their extended families. Unfortunately I had a dizzy spell, another of the ones I had been experiencing over the past few months since Colin died. I came around very quickly, feeling embarrassed but grateful to be among friends. I knew I'd have to see my GP when I got home.

Home was where we were headed the next day. Arlene had bought so many things I had to check some of them with mine.

On the plane, we were lucky to have two seats each. As soon as the captain signalled that it would be safe to unfasten seat belts, Arlene lay down on hers and never spoke to me again on the entire flight home. I'm sure I could have found other friends who would have appreciated being taken on a holiday. To tell the truth I was sorry I had invited Arlene. I couldn't help feeling she had taken advantage of me. However, I knew I'd just have to put it all behind me. As my step mother used to say, "You can't help what you can't change." It had been a good trip in spite of it.

Would coming back to my home without Colin be hard? Well yes, it was, but Lynn and Brett hosted another birthday party for my 80th at the Terminal City Club in Vancouver. When I saw all the family and friends I was weepy for a few minutes. I'd be ok, though, with such great support.

Chapter 14

On My Own Again—Cruising the World

I've met many women who have lost their husbands and they all say much the same thing. The hardest part is getting up in the morning and planning meals for one. It takes self discipline to get up and face the day alone. Even such simple things as reading the morning paper and sharing the news over a cup of coffee or waking up to a lovely day and deciding right then and there to drive out to the country, are no longer possible. The house, not to mention the bed, seems too big for one person. However, I knew in my heart that four husbands were enough for this lady. I had two of the best and as for the others, best not to dwell on past mistakes.

I thought often of the words Colin said to his son shortly before he died. "It's time to go. This is too hard on Margaret." He was in such great pain at the end that it really was a relief to know that his suffering was over. But I missed him so. I missed his cheery wake up call in the morning, his companionship in the garden, his organ playing, enjoying the pool together and the way he appreciated everything I did to make a home for him. He loved my cooking and never failed to thank me at the end of each meal.

I tried to keep this in mind when I returned from my trip to England with Arlene in October. I knew I still had to prove to myself that I could travel on my own or my travelling days would be over. And Colin was right. When I travelled with him I planned the itineraries, arranged for transportation and hotels, purchased the traveller's cheques and packed our clothes.

"Of course you can do it on your own," I told myself. Even so, it was with some misgivings I booked a round the world cruise for January and flew from Vancouver to Istanbul by way of Frankfurt on January 1, 1999.

The family wishes me "Bon voyage!"

The agent who booked my tour told me not to worry when I wanted to make sure that I would have my own room. "The ship is only half full." Somehow I wasn't that reassured, particularly when I found out that it had recently been sold to a Korean shipping company.

It was six o'clock in the evening when, thoroughly tired from more than a day and a half of travel, I finally boarded the *Island Princess*. Two polite young men from the purser's office took me to my very own stateroom.

"So far so good," I thought, remembering what my stepmother used to say.

"Don't go looking for trouble. It will find you soon enough."

If you are a single woman wondering if cruising solo is for you, you are probably wondering if you will either have to sit alone at a table in the dining room or, perhaps worse, be the only single woman sitting at a table of strangers, all of them couples. You needn't worry.

After going to the dining room for something to eat I returned to my room and went straight to bed, not even bothering to unpack. At midnight we would be sailing through the Sea of Marmara. I was glad of an extra blanket because it was cold. I usually pack a warm pair of socks and always a warm sweater that can double as a bed jacket if necessary.

Through the Sea of Marmara, the smallest ocean in the world which connects Europe in the north and Asia in the south, we sailed into the Dardanelles. Early the next afternoon we sailed close by Gallipoli which was a moving experience for me because I had a friend who fought there. He sometimes talked about all the brave souls who perished there in what was surely one of the most mismanaged campaigns of the First World War. Many of the casualties were Australians and New Zealanders. A haunting Australian song, *And the Band Played Waltzing Matilda*, a ballad about the return of an amputee, tells the story of the tragedy of Gallipoli. As the ship sailed past the area, the captain paid a moving tribute to the soldiers.

The ship now sailed southwest through the Aegean Sea. Our next port would be Piraeus. By this time I had met my table mates, all ladies except for one couple, the ship's chaplain, a Catholic priest and Jim, a retired submarine commander. Jim and I hit it off very well. His wife had just passed away and he enjoyed looking after me. I accompanied him on his shopping tours, helping him find just the right gifts for his two sons and daughter. As everyone knows, women far outnumber men on cruises. The ships officers understand that part of their job is social. Most are good company as well as good dancers and conversationalists.

I had been to Athens several times; once as I mentioned earlier, when Colin was hospitalized for several days recovering from food poisoning. As far as I'm concerned there are always good reasons for returning to a place you have visited before. One is to recapture some of the magic of a first time visit; another is to discovered new things, always leaving some room for both in a later visit. Even if your experience in a place was not good, you may find you enjoy it on a second visit. I always keep an open mind and wondered what surprises I would find in Athens this time. The main point of this trip was to reassure myself that I could travel comfortably on my own.

I have found invariably that a single woman can comfortably join any of the sightseeing tours ashore and feel included. It helps if you have a genuine liking for and interest in your fellow passengers. For me it is much like the days when I ran my motel in Kamloops, BC. You meet all types. Sometimes you just click with a person and at the end of the trip you exchange addresses and telephone numbers, vowing to keep in touch. Of course, you don't always follow through, but when as a result of keeping in contact, I find I have links all over the globe, across North American, in England and as far away as Australia.

A group of us decided to hire a driver to take us around the city. I knew, however, that at some point it would be best to do what Ted taught me the first time I saw Athens – go on foot. As the guide provided us aboard the ship advised 'To explore Athens is to walk in the footsteps of those who planted the seeds of Western philosophy, science, culture and art.' The guide neglected to mention that Athens is also a sprawling, noisy, hot city with cement high rises and as much squalor as beauty. A happy tourist knows when to quit and find a good place to sample some local cuisine and wine. We did. Moussaka, lamb kabobs and salad.

Alan Tate, in *The Glories That Are Athens*, talks about the ten top sights in the city. I decided that among my top ten, one of my favourites is the Agora, the ancient answer to the modern shopping mall. It is a long, low roofed promenade, a restoration on the original foundation. I also enjoyed seeing the handsome ceremonial guards in their pleated miniskirts outside the Parliament building. Our driver took us to the flea market with its lanes and alleys filled with shops selling everything from clothes and shoes to brassware and pottery.

"Don't forget to bargain," my new friend Jim reminded us. "They expect a little haggling."

This summer, when I watched the Olympic Games on television, it was an opportunity for a little armchair travel to this 4,000 year-old city.

Good and tired at the end of the day, I was glad to be aboard ship again to shower away the grit and grime of Athens, ready for a cruise through the Greek Islands on our way to Ashdod and the Holy Land.

Ashdod is the second port of Israel. Its artificial harbour is protected from sea swells by curved breakwaters a mile long. An industrial city today, it was an early Christian centre.

A bus took us to Jerusalem from Ashdod. Jerusalem, a city whose roots go back to the fourth millennium, BCE, is a sacred site to more than a third of the earth's monotheistic religions. It is the sacred city of Jews, Christians and Muslims. The old walled city is divided into four quarters, Muslim, Jewish, Armenian and Christian. The wall is said to contain a piece of Solomon's temple.

I couldn't believe I was in the city where Christ was crucified. Quite likely this city had a spiritual quality about it but didn't seem quite real to me in my Sunday school days. Now I tried to imagine the Jewish temple which was destroyed by the Romans in 70 CE. Here I was, standing perhaps in the Garden of Gethsemane on the Mount of Olives with its very ancient olive trees, visiting the Church of the Holy Sepulcher, walking in the steps of Christ and his followers.

Seeing the Wailing Wall was another experience I will never forget. All the sorrows the Jewish people have endured throughout history seemed embodied in that spot.

Although there has been so much bloodshed in this area it was relatively quiet as we boarded our tour bus headed for Bethlehem. I read recently that this town, during Jesus' lifetime, was a thriving and sophisticated cultural centre. It was also Ruth's home and the site of Rachel's tomb as well as the supposed birth place of Jesus. Looking down from a hill over fertile farmland and the Dead Sea in the distance, it relied on the then steady stream of pilgrims and tourists. Most of the inhabitants are Christians. The excellent museum celebrates Bethlehem's cultural heritage, with exhibits of clothing, household items and old photographs. The Church of the Nativity, which was not actually built until four centuries after Christ's death, also has a spiritual quality to it.

One great aspect of tour travel is, that if it is a good

tour, you will always be fed and bedded down well. Our lunch in Jerusalem, in one of the city's very modern hotels, was lovely. Fresh fruit and a crisp salad with good bread revived all of us at mid day. Back on the ship for dinner that evening meant a more excellent food, good conversation and a good night's sleep.

Looking at my itinerary the next morning, I learned that our next stop would be Port Said, known to ocean liner passengers as the 'Gateway to the East'. Founded in 1858 and named for the Egyptian khedive, Said Pasha, it is on the Mediterranean entrance to the Suez Canal. It is built on an artificial promontory where the Nile delta meets the marsh and sand of the Sinai Peninsula and, while the town is relatively new, its history as an agricultural area goes back to the time of the pharaohs. Travellers through the canal, as well as on trips down the Nile, pass through it. Visitors from Cairo shop duty free here.

A three hour bus ride took us across the desert to view the pyramids of Giza, the last remaining wonder of the ancient world. That bus ride across the desert gave me quite a different perspective from the last time I visited these massive stone structures when we approached them by air.

The purser is like the head steward on a passenger liner. This means looking after the comfort and welfare of the passengers, including providing a staff member from the ship's company to accompany single passengers off the ship if required. Sightseeing alone was something I knew I could do but to which I didn't look forward. I needn't have worried. This time I was accompanied by a nice young man who was seeing Egypt for the first time. It was fun being a tour guide for him, telling him about the important artifacts in the museum in Cairo and the ancient history of the area.

"Did you ever think you would be here in Egypt?" I asked him. Of course seeing the world was just one of the reasons this young man had signed on the ship. Once again

Margaret riding a well-dressed camel

I proved that, even at 80, I could still ride a camel, although I chose not to go into the pyramid.

While we were seeing the sights, our ship was in a holding area waiting to enter the canal when we returned. Each ship going through the canal has to demonstrate that its anchors are in good working order by raising and lowering them in successive anchorages. Ships pass through the canal in single lanes of traffic, separated by one mile. In case of engine or steering failures the anchors serve as brakes. The south bound convoys head to the Great Bitter Lake, take up assigned anchorages and wait for the north bound convoy to pass and then continue. The canal is over 100 miles long and can accommodate ships with a maximum draft of fifty-three feet.

I was thrilled to be going through and stood on the upper deck for the whole time. It was a beautiful day, the Egyptian side so green in contrast to the Sinai's desert sand. The tiny strip of land, known in the Bible as Goshen, is bridged by the canal to connect the Mediterranean and the Red Sea, thus creating a passage way between Asia and Africa. Many attempts have been made to connect these bodies of water, some as far back as 9th century BCE. Xerxes, Ptolemy and Trajan all were responsible for construction before it finally fell into disrepair around the 8th century CE. It is said that Napoleon considered rebuilding the waterway but in the end abandoned the idea. Finally in the 1850s the French engineer, Ferdinand de Lesseps, was granted permission by Said Pasha to begin construction. Britain purchased the largest shares in the undertaking. When the canal was finally opened there was a grand celebration with royalty from around the world. Verdi wrote his opera, Aida, for the opening of the new Cairo opera house. All the major powers of the world agreed that the canal would be neutral territory and guaranteed safe passage of any ship in peace or wartime.

In fact, it was eventually returned to Egypt by the major shareholders in the Suez Canal Company, Britain and the U.S. Trouble broke out when Israel, who had been denied passage through the canal for eight years and who had been attacked by Egypt along its border, invaded Egypt. Britain and France sent troops to retake the canal but in the end the United Nations emergency forces replaced these troops. The canal was closed for six months and it was necessary to clear it of debris and sunken ships. The Egyptians would not allow access to Israeli vessels and the canal was closed again by Egypt during the Arab-Israeli War. Strife between Israel and Egypt continued until 1975. US forces stepped in at that time to once again clear the canal of debris. Now huge dredges keep busy pumping sand, which blows in from the desert, out of certain areas in the canal.

As we entered the Red Sea we passed a beautiful mosque on our right side and saw many container ships piled so high I wondered how they kept afloat. Then, as we sailed down through the sea, we were soon out of sight of land, later passing through the narrow straight that separates the Red Sea from the Gulf of Aden. Suddenly we were treated to the spectacle of flying fish. Local fishermen catch these at night by shining flashlights on the sails of their boats. The fish, 10-12 inches long, fly into the sails and drop into the boats. They have brilliant silvery scales which sparkle as they fly. They can actually fly distances from 20 to 200 yards. I stood enthralled at schools of them appeared to take flight, pursued by larger fish.

The sea was very calm as we sailed towards our next port, Oman. The captain took the opportunity to give us landlubbers another lesson in maritime terminology. That day the subject was the crow's nest. In the early days of the sailing ships they always carried a coop of land birds high in the mast. If winds carried the ship out of sight of land, the birds would be released so the captain could follow them to shore. Later a barrel or platform high in the mast served as a lookout for one of the sailors.

Oman, with its landscape of scenic mountains and long, unspoiled beaches, proved a pleasant surprise. Instead of touring Muscat, the capital, we toured Oman's

Oman,
January 13ᵗʰ, 1999

second city, Salalah, the only corner of the region favoured by the Indian summer monsoon. This means the city enjoys a cool, wet and green summer just as the rest of the region swelters under the worst of the season's heat. Oman impressed me as a very clean city, its streets lined with royal palms. We visited some of the bazaars which sold fresh fruits and perfumes. I remember noticing that the women walked about freely, none wearing the traditional burkas covering their faces. We understood that a treat was in store for archaeology buffs and I thought immediately of Ted, my second husband. I imagined how thrilled he would have been as we were driven into the mountains to see Job's tomb. It is over 4,000 years old! We also saw the incense trees from which frankincense is derived.

That night the ship headed across the Arabian Sea towards our next stop, Bombay, or Mumbai as it is now known. We learned from the ship's guide that this city of 13 million people is full of contrasts, both fabulously rich and terribly poor. Sky-scrapers stand side by side with graceful Victorian buildings which hearken back to the British India of the Raj. Sports cars race down the streets beside horse drawn carriages. Mumbai has sunny beaches, an exciting nightlife, fashionable shops and colourful bazaars.

Once a tropical archipelago of seven islands and the Raj's brightest jewel, Mumbai was part of the dowry of Portuguese Princess Infanta Catherine de Braganza who married Charles II of England in 1661.

As we entered the harbour we passed through a fleet of fishing boats, both purse seiners and drift net boats. We were welcomed by a brass band in full dress uniform.

The day was hot and humid as we boarded our bus for a tour of the city. Along the way we stopped to watch women washing clothes by hand in wash tubs, something they have been doing for years. I was surprised that the clothes came out very white —something I commented on after seeing women beating clothes in the Nile. Evidently they don't need super power detergents!

It was so hot I welcomed our next stop, a beautiful garden filled with topiary in many animal shapes built on top of a reservoir but I was not looking forward to the next place on our itinerary, the Elephant Caves. I made myself enter with the rest of our group and was glad I did. Carved from rock sometime in the 6th century, the caves were filled with statues of the Hindu gods.

Beyond the imperial city of Agra is one of the truly fabulous sights in the world, the Taj Mahal, a mausoleum built by the Mogul emperor Shah Jahan for his beloved wife. Everyone who visits the site is awed by its beauty and nearly everyone wants a photograph standing before the reflecting pool. Inside, light filters through intricately carved screens set high in the walls. The Taj Mahal, as befitting its status of a world heritage monument, is in impeccably good condition.

Later on that day we visited the home of Mahatma Ghandi, the father of modern India. I was distressed by the many begging children and wasn't sorry to leave. I have read since that forty percent of India's taxes come from Mumbai and that millionaires and paupers are made overnight. I found it hard to accept that there was so much wealth in evidence and yet so much poverty.

Our ship took us away from Mumbai on a flooding tide, heading south along the coast of India towards the port of Cochin, only 10 degrees north of the equator. We would be passing Mangalore and Calcutta before stopping in Cochin. On our first clear dark night aboard we looked down over the water to see 'glow-in-the-dark' dolphins playing. A phenomenon that occurs in these waters is bioluminescence, once known as phosphorescence because it is similar to the effect caused when phosphorous is exposed to oxygen.

Cochin's ancient and multicultural heritage is reflected in its population and in its varied architectural styles today. Jewish synagogues, Portuguese churches, Dutch mansions and houses on stilts greet the visitor beyond the docks and the 'godowner' warehouses along the waterfront. Words have always fascinated me and I had heard this term 'godownder' once before in California. I asked a young man there what he did for a living. "I'm a godowner," he responded, and when I asked him what that meant, he said it was an East Indian term for someone who fetches this and that. I guess most of us have been 'godowners' from time to time.

We learned that very little has changed in this old city since Europeans settled here in the 1500s. It is believed to be the oldest European settlement in India but its history reaches far back to the time of King Solomon. He stopped here, according to legend, a thousand years BCE in search of materials to build the first Hebrew temple in Jerusalem.

Heading south, down the western coast of India, our next port of call would be Singapore. Our captain explained that we'd be crossing the Bay of Bengal, passing the tip of Sri Lanka and sailing through the Malacca Strait which links the Indian Ocean with the South China Sea.

"You'll see all kinds of water vessels as we head down the Strait," he told us. "It's a navigational challenge because we have to maintain the correct depth for the ship and be ever vigilant to avoid hitting another ship. It's the ocean version of a traffic jam." I was looking forward to seeing Singapore again.

In the meantime, it was a case of what to do when there's nothing to do. I always take along my current needlework project and some good books, hoping that the ship has a swimming pool. I just sit back and take it easy with no meals to plan and cook (always a challenge when you are single), no beds to make, no housework and no gardening. When I'm at home I have plenty of all of these to keep me busy from morning to night.

Singapore is truly one of my favourite cities in the world. To start with, unlike many East Asian cities, it is impeccably clean. Citizens and tourists alike are aware that littering is against the law as is spitting. Also, Singapore, like Cochin, reflects its history of cultural diversity from its modern glass and steel skyscrapers, Victorian government buildings, red roofed Chinese shops and Buddhist temples to its Middle Eastern bazaars.

Singapore proper is actually a main island surrounded by 63 smaller islands. Our captain told us that it is the busiest port in the world with over 600 shipping lines using the port facilities every year. Watching from the deck as we entered the port we saw super tankers and container and cruise ships. It is mentioned in Chinese writings as far back as the 3rd century. Just as today one sees a wide variety of vessels in port, in former days Portuguese battleships, Arab dhows, Chinese junks and schooners filled the harbour. Over the centuries the name of the city name changed from Temasek (sea town) to Singa Pura (lion town). In the early 1800s the British realized that the port would make a strategic centre for refitting and provisioning their growing fleet in the Far East. Sir Stamford Raffles established Singapore not only as a free trade station for merchants from across Asia and the Middle East, but to prevent advances from the Dutch in the area. The Dutch and British East India companies continued rivalry throughout the 1800s.

Margaret and Jim exploring Raffles

Singapore's history as a British protectorate remained peaceful until the Japanese invaded the country in the Second World War. After the war it became a Crown Colony, gaining independence as a republic in 1965.

Our trip ashore included a cricket match and a visit to the world famous Raffles Hotel, named after the first British governor of Singapore. Located at 1 Beach Road and advertising itself as 'Patronized by nobility, loved by all', it was declared a national monument and completely remodelled and restored in 1991. Raffles began as a beach house with bentwood tables and rattan chairs. It now has 19 bars and restaurants, a spa and pool, over 50 shops, a theatre and a club for children. It also has a florist shop elegantly named *Sir Charles, Flowers for the Gentlemen* and a gourmet food shop. For my part, I loved the old world charm of the place, one of the world's grand hotels with crystal chandeliers and beautiful gardens.

Sitting in the Long Bar and enjoying the legendary Singapore Sling is a must. Created by Mr. Ngiam Tong Boon for the hotel sometime before the First World War, it was originally created as a ladies' drink. The recipe, locked away by Mr. Tong Boon and later written down by a visitor on a bar chit, is somewhat disputed. For those wishing to try it at home, here is a version courtesy of drinkboy.com.

1 1/2 oz. gin	*4 oz. pineapple juice*
½ oz. Cherry Herring brandy	*½ oz. lime juice*
¼ oz. Cointreau	*1/3 oz. grenadine*
¼ oz. Dom Benedictine	*dash Angostura Bitters*

Garnish with a slice of pineapple and cherry

Enjoy as we did!

Later, my friend Jim suggested with a twinkle in his eye, "Let's explore behind that sign, pointing to 'Private – Guests Only Past This Point'. Trying to look like guests we walked around the sign and explored some of the halls. It was, after all, only a hotel. We could not see the guest rooms.

Leaving Singapore, watching over the ship's rails as we headed south east down the Strait of Malacca, we could understand the captain's need for vigilance. We observed smaller ships crossing lanes and making

U-turns while pilots manoeuvred vessels to and from the port. Heading into the South China Sea, we watched the waters become even busier as we threaded through all manner of fishing vessels, large and small.

We were headed for Kuantan on the east of the Malay Peninsula, a magical place. Ancient traditions are honoured and practised there daily. Since 2000 BCE, the Chinese, Buddhists, Brahmans, Hindus and finally the Dutch and the British established themselves here. Aboriginals still inhabit the jungles and hills. According to the Lonely Planet guide, Malaysia is still one of the most pleasant and hassle-free countries to visit in South-East Asia, where many cultures live side by side. We wandered through sleepy little villages, watched the locals fishing from brightly painted boats with gracefully carved prows, and tried our hand at the local sport, top spinning. It is harder than it looks.

Separated from the western peninsula by vast stands of rain forest and rugged mountains, the eastern coast has many long stretches of unspoiled sandy beaches. The friendly people enjoy a simple way of life.

Too soon we were back on board ship, heading northward to the Gulf of Thailand. The high, wooded off shore islands make this a scenic trip. Our destination was Thailand's only major seaport, Samut Sakhon. It is also a busy fishing centre which provides Bangkok with fresh fish, daily. Our bus took us from there into Bangkok, on the Chao Phraya River, truly one of the most magnificent cities of the world. There we all trouped aboard a ferry to the floating market. Hundreds of small boats along the klong displayed fresh fruits and vegetables as well as fish, chicken and other meats. Flimsy houses, adequate shelter in the 96 degree temperature, lined the canal. We watched strings of barges being loaded for sea going ships or warehouses. We stopped for lunch at the old Erewan Hotel and then we were off in a combination of heat and humidity for the Royal Palace.

It may be a cliché, but you can't help thinking about the musical, *Anna and the King of Siam* when you enter this fairyland of spires, its walls inlaid with glass, porcelain and gold. The real Anna, Anna Leowens, was a spunky widow who took her children with her when she became a governess to the King of Siam's children. You could almost hear *Getting to Know You* and *I Whistle a Happy Tune* echoing through the highly decorated chambers. While you can detect European influence in the Royal Palace, the Thais are fiercely proud of the fact that their country remained independent while so many other areas around them fell under the influence of the major colonial empires of the British, French and Dutch.

I've said that my first husband, Ted, was a good teacher. He believed in reading all you can about a place before you actually visit it. I had done my homework before we took off our shoes to enter the Temple of the Emerald Buddha. Legend has it that this statue, thought to be made of stucco, was found to be made of jade when the abbot of the temple where it was housed, noticed that the stucco had flaked off the nose. The king tried three times unsuccessfully to move the statue to Chiangmai from Lampang. Three times the elephant carrying it ran away. The king took this to be a sign that the Buddha should remain where it was. However, a succession of rulers did move the Buddha before it finally found its present home in 1784. The statue has three seasonal costumes which only the king is allowed to change. The ceremony takes place in the rainy, summer and winter seasons.

At the end of the day, our heads filled with exotic images, it was good to return to the hotel for a refreshing shower and a change of clothing. I do a quick wash of all my clothes every night when I travel, carrying only things that dry quickly. Then I change before the night's activities. A quick nap before dinner helps too, although I hate to use travel time on too much sleep. You know, when you are on a tour that you need to get to bed relatively early because the next day's activities seem to start a few minutes after you put your head on your pillow. Touring is not for sissies.

Night time in Bangkok is exciting but can be dangerous too, and this is another reason for a single woman to travel on a guided tour. You can enjoy a bit of nightlife without worrying about petty theft or worse. Thailand, like many other destinations in the world, can be dangerous due to terrorism. Even some Buddhist temples have been bombed and public transportation is not safe for women alone. Hotel rooms should be locked and bolted at night and a woman should not use any taxis but those with yellow and black licence plates. The guided tour is now the only way I travel.

On our last night in Bangkok we enjoyed a nightclub with lovely Thai dancing girls. The next morning we'd be on our way up the Mekong to Ho Chi Minh City.

It unnerved me right form the start. We had travelled up the shallow Saigon River, jungle on both banks. Vietnam was colonized by the French before the US sent troops into the country in 1965. Ho Chi Minh City, formerly Saigon, still reflects its French colonial past. The French drained the marshlands upon which the city now stands. It is home to over ten million inhabitants. I was looking forward to the street markets, sidewalk cafes and shops. However there was so much noise; cars, motorcycles and bicycles whizzing by at dizzying speeds.

When our bus stopped at a temple I found myself unwilling to get out so I stayed on board. Usually on tours you are somewhat sheltered from beggers and hucksters but not this time. Before long an old lady in rags with a bucket was knocking on my window. I knew there was a wide, wide gulf between us, not just a pane of glass. I thought how different our lives were and felt inexplicably threatened.

After leaving the temple we had a lunch of exotic fruit while watching the river, packed with boats. We travelled back to the city, seeing women working in the rice paddies and many water buffalo.

Lunch on tour

Who could resist this Vietnamese child?

I was glad to leave Vietnam, with its history of war and suffering. Our last sight of the country was the jagged cliffs and windswept sand hills along its central coast. We were headed for the South China Sea.

I was looking forward to our next stop, Hong Kong. I had been there before and, while I found the cacophony of Ho Chi Minh City threatening, I knew I'd love the familiar hustle and bustle of Hong Kong. I looked at the map and saw that we'd be entering via the Lantau Channel. The pilot joining us at Junk Island would guide the ship into our berth on Hong Kong Island. I loved the excitement of standing on deck as we entered the harbour. Soon we could see Victoria Peak on one side and then all the skyscrapers of this great lively city on the other. The harbour was filled with sampans and junks. I was hungry. A Scottish band piped us to our berth. Many a junk is home to an entire family including pets and livestock, so you see kids, flowerpots and cooking going on aboard. The sights and smell of the cooking reminded me of how long I'd been standing on deck watching the activity. I was hungry! Our dinner that night would be at the Aberdeen Floating Restaurant so I hurried below to shower and dress.

The restaurant was pagoda-like, twinkling with outdoor lights and the menu, mainly Chinese, included live fish and other seafood, cooked for you of course. Very fresh.

I was eager to walk on Nathan Road, one of the main shopping streets in Hong Kong. I soon noticed that prices had increased since I'd been there last. I couldn't resist a string of pearls.

Jim and I took a harbour cruise before we prepared to leave the city.

We were bound for the 7,000 islands of the Philippines, stretching across the 115,000 square miles between the South China Sea and the Pacific Ocean. This was also familiar territory because I had been there with Ted. I wondered what changes I would find as we entered Manila Bay.

The stop here included a Tagatay Tour. We passed more rice paddies and coconut groves, stopping at Las Pinas Church for an organ recital. The organist was an Irishman with a thick brogue. He played on a 196 year old bamboo organ. Later we drove past the salt beds, water evaporating from them in the hot sun and then on to Lake Taal to view an active volcano. From there we had a panoramic view of the mountains and farmland below.

Lunch was Philippine style including young green coconuts filled with ice cream. Delicious! At the end of the day we visited the US Memorial Cemetery. There are 18,000 crosses and 36,000 names inscribed in the rotunda. On entering Manila Bay we had passed the Bataan Peninsula and Corregidor Island where, during the Second World War, American and Philippine troops under General Douglas MacArthur tried unsuccessfully to stave off the Japanese.

The next day we put on our bathing suits, mine under my sundress. Our destination was the Pagsanjan Falls. Along the way we saw women planting rice seedlings, washing in small streams and hanging laundry to dry in the sun, gossiping among themselves. We then seated ourselves in small narrow solid wooden boats paddled by young men. They literally forced our way up the rapids to the falls by sheer muscle power. The walls of the river rose 300 feet on both sides, covered with luxurious growth, vines and ferns entangled in the jungle trees. When we arrived at the falls we boarded a bamboo raft which took us behind the falls through a misty veil of water. The falls dropped two hundred feet in two steps. It was fun but wet!

After lunch, our return trip took us past more rice fields, small villages, water buffalo, green fields, horse-drawn carriages, colourful jitneys and vegetable stalls with rice cakes and steaming corn for sale. The day ended with a tour of the Presidential Palace. There were beautiful chandeliers and wood carvings but no sign of the shoe collection of Imelda Marcos, the former President's wife.

Sadly, we saw many unemployed Philippinos. They stood at the harbour hoping to get work on ships like ours. Many of the women try desperately to get work in Canada and the US and are often badly treated, underpaid and overworked. Yet, in spite of everything, they manage to send money to families back home. This money is taxed by the Phillippine government.

As we neared the equator, those of us who had crossed this imaginary line before wondered what ceremony would mark this crossing. This time King Neptune and his court of mermaids officiated. Our captain got dunked many times, the guests on board helping with the fun. The poor man was doused with whipped cream, catsup, green jelly, parmesan cheese and spaghetti. It was a complete mess but good fun and the captain took it all with good grace. This ceremony is so old that its origin has been lost. In the Royal Navy it is the custom to initiate those who have not crossed the equator before. It was a perfect day but way too hot for me. Some folks who tan easily seem to tolerate the sun but I guess I'm just too fair skinned. I find the shade.

The next morning found me looking at my map, desperately trying to find Buton in Sulawesi. We were supposed to go to Ambon but, because of civil unrest there, Captain Oliver announced that the ship's course would take us to Buton instead. Fighting between Muslims and Christians has made this an unsafe destination for tourists to this day. Maluku Province, once known by its romantic name, the Spice Islands, has been the scene of brawls where rival mobs have fought with swords, bows and arrows and gasoline bombs. "A place to avoid," one of my table mates put succinctly at dinner. In fact, in recent months, with terrorist activities common throughout the area, you will not find me anywhere near there.

I could see on the map that we would be sailing past the Sulu Archipelago to the Sulu Sea, passing the islands of Negros and Manado, through a narrow channel into the Celebes Sea. Manado, in northern Sulawesi, is a real tropical paradise with millions of coconut palms. It is very mountainous with some active volcanoes. It was once 'owned' by the Portuguese who were expelled by the Dutch.

We sailed through many islands, from coral atolls peeping through blue water to large land masses spewed forth from volcanoes, some recently active. As we rounded Lembeh Island I was on deck watching for the first sight of Buton, once a thriving depot between trade in the islands of East Indonesia, Java and Europe. Dancing natives welcomed us in fancy masks and colourful costumes made from the feathers of the island's exotic birds.

We were bound for Australia.

Shall we dance? Jim and Margaret

We had a day at sea after leaving Buton. A typical day at sea for me started with a wake-up call at 7. Everyone received an information sheet each morning telling about shipboard events including lectures and describing the day's passage. We also received information about the next port of call, including tours available. Jim and I breakfasted together and then promenaded the deck. I would usually read or do my needlework - on this trip a picture of a thatched cottage-have a swim and write in my travel journal. The journal serves more than one purpose. I like to remember the trip details when I'm home again and it also serves to help me identify my photos. The journals I've kept over the years helped me to write this book.

There were often lectures in the afternoon. One of the lecturers on this trip was Sir Arnold Wolfendale, the 14th Astronomer Royal. He lectured on the night sky and also on the pyramids. This cruise also offered history lectures on board, particularly if we would not be putting into a port that day. I found these sessions excellent because they made the trip so much more interesting.

My schooling was cut short when I was only fifteen so I really like to take advantage of the opportunity to fill in the gaps. They also help you to get acquainted with your fellow passengers. I have no patience with folks who either spend the whole time on board playing card games, or, worse still, gambling in the casinos.

This day we learned about Captain Cook, the Yorkshire man with an aptitude for math, navigation and mapmaking. Every school child in British Columbia learns about him and his expeditions to the northwest coast of the province. First apprenticed to shipbuilders in Whitby, early in his career he earned a reputation as a surveyor. Upon joining the Royal Navy he made expeditions to the Saint Lawrence, Newfoundland and Labrador. In August, 1768 he set forth from Plymouth. Reaching Rio de Janeiro and rounding Cape Horn, he arrived in Tahiti the next spring. This expedition was for exploration as well as being for scientific purposes. The voyage was sponsored by a wealthy patron, Joseph Banks, who brought along eight servants, a Swedish botanist and an astronomer. Navigational calculations, done without any of the modern instruments for measuring longitude, were based on lunar data and charts which Cook had made on earlier voyages.

Our shipboard teacher explained that Cook charted the islands through which we would soon be sailing. The sea that day was very calm and as we were a small group, we were by now very comfortable with each other. I was also feeling more confident about my ability to mix with relative strangers without Colin. This might seem a contradiction since I have mentioned that he was quite a shy man. Somehow, though, he gave me confidence.

By that evening we were headed towards Cape Wessel, following a well-charted route. Our teacher explained that a shorter route would be through waters for which, surprisingly in this technological era, the charts were too old to be considered reliable. I thought to myself, "I guess they were not made by Captain Cook."

Almost every night on this trip we were treated to lovely floorshows. One night we had new lead singers, Lelani Marrell and Tony Gats from West Vancouver. At first I dreaded these evenings. Both Ted and Colin loved to dance but now, without an escort, I was not sure what the protocol would be. However, I remember how nice Ted was when there were single women seated with us in the evening on cruises. He was very generous, always buying a round of drinks. I grew up in a time when women didn't go into bars and night clubs alone. I had never even been into a liquor store until after Ted died.

The next morning our ship headed east across the Gulf of Carpentaria towards Torres Strait and finally to the Great Barrier Reef. We entered the Great Barrier Reef at midnight. Navigation in these waters is very difficult. The reef extends over 1000 miles off the east coast of Australia. Although it was too dark to see, we passed a cave at which, early in the 1900s, sailors would drop off supplies for ship wrecked mariners. Passage along the great coral reef is difficult at the best of times but this particular trip was very stormy. We were running ahead of a cyclone. I prayed that we would not be among those shipwrecked along this coast. Some of the passengers were seasick. Almost all of us were apprehensive if not downright terrified. Five hundred and seventy miles later we were within sight of Cairns on the south end of Trinity Bay, Queensland's most northerly city. The bay was named by Captain Cook who anchored there on Trinity Sunday, 1770.

I had been looking forward to a trip out to the Great Barrier Reef. Several of us had our bathing suits on and our beach bags packed with towels and sun screen. But the weather was still too stormy, the Captain informed us as he headed the ship towards Brisbane, some 800 miles away. The sea remained very choppy. The cyclone now had a name, Roma. Although disappointed, we all were glad we would still be keeping ahead of trouble.

After a day and night at sea, we arrived in Brisbane where we picked up a local pilot shortly after breakfast. He would guide us through the many banks, shoals and shallows which are a feature of Moreton Bay, finally berthing our liner on the north banks of the Brisbane River.

Brisbane, the capital of Queensland, grew up along this river. The city planners wisely kept many of the old historical buildings which somehow mix gracefully with the new modern ones. We left the ship for a trip to a koala sanctuary and then a drive through the city to its highest spot. The bears are soft and cuddly and don't seem to mind being snuggled. Later we had a real English tea with scrumptious scones and strawberry jam and cups of hot, refreshing tea.

Margaret and a cuddly companion

A buffet lunch

Speaking of eating and drinking, I'm usually very careful on cruises not to gain weight. It is a real temptation on board to overeat. There is so much food presented so attractively but alas, high in calories, it is hard to resist. It takes all my will power to resist the urge to overeat. I try to keep active by walking and swimming and once in a while I give in!

St. Valentine's Day would be celebrated on board before we reached Sidney, our next stop. On the evening every lady on board received a bouquet of red roses. This was the first time my Valentine flowers were not accompanied by a note saying, "With all my love, Colin".

213

I was determined not to feel sorry for myself. I wasn't the only woman travelling alone. It is a fact of life that as women age, they far outnumber men. Besides, Jim and I got along very well together and he was there for me on this special night for lovers.

Next morning nearly all the revellers were on deck. The day dawned clear and sunny, the storm clouds and choppy seas behind us, as we steamed into the harbour. Sidney's shimmering skyline greeted us. We could see both the bridge, which the natives call the coat hanger, and the famous opera house. I had a special treat in store.

Tana Davies, the sister of Colin's son-in-law, was waiting to show me her city. First we would visit the opera house, and then have coffee before a tour of the city's fabled beaches. Finally we would have lunch in a revolving restaurant high above the harbour where we could see the city laid out before us. Sidney was bustling with preparations for the Olympics. It was an exciting time. Late in the afternoon, after some shopping, Tana took me back to her place to meet her daughter Tamara and her son Brett. We had a lovely dinner.

I think it is delightful when someone like Tana shows you their city. You really get an insider's view of a place in a way no guided tour can. I often do this for friends visiting Vancouver. I show them my favourite places and then bring them home for a West Coast dinner featuring a salmon barbecue, in-season vegetables and a berry pie.

I went to bed that night relaxed and happy to be heading for Tasmania after writing a thank you note to Tana for such a fine day.

The Tasman Sea was rough and it was raining and much cooler when we arrived in Hobart the next morning around 9 o'clock. I decided that Storm Bay is aptly named and was glad I had packed some warm clothes. Layering is the secret. You can always remove a layer or two if you are too hot.

An organized tour took us into Hoehn Valley to a wild life park. The countryside reminded me of my home in British Columbia, with pine and fir trees, apple orchards and vineyards. We stopped for a tour of a very modern winery and then went on to meet the famous Tasmanian devils. These are bear-like marsupial carnivores that look cute until they open their mouths. One bite from those sharp teeth equals a two-ton chomp!

We had lunch at a quaint country inn. It was more dinner than lunch, featuring oysters, scallops and salmon, new potatoes and fresh mushrooms accompanied by local beer. For dessert we had plump raspberries and thick cream. I'd have to cut back on dinner or I'd need a new wardrobe at this rate.

Following the lunch we viewed the largest catamaran in the world, built in Hobart. A few days at sea again stretched out before us until we reached Fremantle and Perth.

It was time for another history lesson. We had, by now, almost circumnavigated the continent of Australia. "Does anyone know the origin of the name Australia?" our teacher asked.

Geographers in the classical world knew the earth was a sphere. There must be a land mass on the other side of the world, they reasoned, to balance off the continents of Europe and Asia. This imagined land mass was named on the maps of the time as Terra Australis which meant southern land.

That morning the class reviewed the seven seas, a term which used to mean all the waters of the earth. The seven specifically are the Arctic and Antarctic, the north and south Pacific and Atlantic and the Indian oceans.

Freemantle is the port for Perth, the capital of Western Australia, about fifteen miles up the Swan River. It is another bright city which has blended modern buildings with historic old sandstone ones. The Swan River does have its swans, stately black ones swimming on the river which is named for them. We stopped at King's Park, largely untouched bush, for another lovely tea in beautiful gardens atop Mount Eliza. From there we could see Perth spread out before us.

I'd lost count of the number of days we had been at sea. We were bound, across the southern part of one of those seas we had learned about, the Indian Ocean, to the island of Mauritius. The next morning I looked out my stateroom window to see birds, a sure sign that we were nearing land. As usual we picked up our pilot who would take us into Port Louis.

Mauritius was uninhabited until the 16th century when Dutch, British and French traders came to the island, followed by African slaves and Indian labourers. Today it is predominantly French. We would spend the day touring two botanical gardens, always a favourite activity of mine. One was the Sir Seewoosagur Ramgoolan, the other the Jardin des Pamplemousses, the grapefruit garden. Among the weird and wonderful trees we saw that day was the blood tree, named because in summer it oozes a red sap. There was also a palm tree that blooms only once in sixty years and then dies.

That night we celebrated New Year's with a party on deck under a full moon, two months late! With paper streamers and champagne we danced a great Conga line. We were on our way to Reunion Island, some 400 miles east of the island of Madagascar. Even with all that partying I was up early to catch sight of this breathtaking place of natural beauty. From a distance it looked like a green emerald, with lush mountains and volcanic peaks. Its beaches are sandy, white or black from the active volcanoes, the latest of which erupted in 1998. Reunion Island is also known for its vanilla production so we were off to Vanilla House. Our drive took us into a lush canyon with tree fern and phoenix bamboo, which I hadn't seen since my trip to southern China with Colin in 1985. We passed many waterfalls along the way.

Vanilla is the product of the vanilla orchid. The process of pollination of this flower by hand was discovered by botanist Edmond Albus, in 1841. The reason we pay such a high price for vanilla is the lengthy process of first extracting the vanilla and then drying it for a long time in the sun before crushing it.

I was suddenly aware I hadn't made the transition into the latest time zone. On the drive I just couldn't stay awake. Perhaps all that sea air was finally getting to me. Perhaps I was finally letting go, accepting my new life. That night I slept soundly and dreamlessly. Durban and Cape Town lay ahead.

I recalled the last time I had been to these two South African cities with Ted. Thanks to our friends Mitzi and Edward, we had seen the insider's South Africa. As I wrote in my first book, it was a perfect holiday until Edward asked Ted to smuggle a large sum of money out of the country. Of course Ted refused. I knew that Edward and Mitzi had since immigrated to Ireland and wondered what had happened to them since.

Durban attracts hundreds of thousands of visitors each year. This time we were whisked past the Golden Mile, really a stretch of three and a half miles of sandy beach, hotels, amusement parks and restaurants. Instead we went to Kwazulu, where at Shakaland, we were treated to the pulsating rhythms of Zulu drummers and dancers.

We were nearing the end of this fabulous cruise as

we rounded Cape Natal along the South African coast. It is known as the Romantic Coast for its magnificent beaches. The port of East London was originally a supply centre for the military stationed in nearby King William's Town. Now it is a large industrial hub, manufacturing textiles, wool and electronic components.

I wondered if Cape Town had changed very much. It was, after all, more than twenty years since I last visited it and much had occurred in the country since then. From the ship I could see Table Mountain, Devil's Peak and Lion's Head. It was time for another shipboard history lesson.

On a fateful day in April, 1652, the Dutch merchant Jan Van Reebeck dropped anchor at Table Bay and hoisted the flag of the Dutch East India Company. Settlers built a walled earthen fort and soon fruit and vegetable gardens were established. This would be a shelter from the often stormy seas off the Cape, provide fruit, vegetables, wine and meat for settlers and sailors, provide care for the sick and enable repairs for ships.

Before the arrival of the Dutch, others lived in the area, cattle herders, hunters of the bountiful game and beach combers who searched the shores for seafood. Very few clues remain of their existence, fragments of ancient tools and myths handed down through generations. Legends were told of visitors from afar. Phoenician sailors and Arab adventurers such as Sinbad the Sailor may have washed up on these shores.

I was seeing this peninsula from quite a different perspective than the last time I visited the country, when I was looking at the sea from the beach. We could expect to see all kinds of sea creatures; penguins, porpoises, sharks, whales, seals and walruses, many seabirds such as gannets and even an albatross.

I expected to see changes in Cape Town. It had always seemed such a romantic place, a blend of eastern and western cultures as well as African. Countless ships arrive every year. Some of them are too large for easy docking and these are serviced by helicopters. Since the end of apartheid there has been much unrest. I hoped that South Africans would learn to live at peace with each other in this beautiful country.

I flew straight from Cape Town to London where Connie met me and took me home for a typical English breakfast of sausages, bacon, eggs, toast and jam and a pot of tea. "Honestly, Connie," I said, "the hardest part of these past three months has been pushing myself away from the table. It's a good thing I'm on my way home."

"You'll soon be back to normal," she laughed. After a hot shower and a nap she drove me to the airport for my flight home.

"I was worried about you, Margaret," she said as she hugged me goodbye, "but I can see you are going to be just fine. This trip has done you a world of good."

A ton of mail awaited me when I walked in the door.

"Well," I thought, "I guess this is where the rest of my life begins. I think I can handle it." I could have sworn that Colin's picture on the wall winked at me.

Chapter 15

On a Riverboat in France

When I arrived home from my world cruise, one of the first things I did was to call my friend Gladys Wright. Her husband had not been well for quite some time and I wondered how they both were. I was sorry to hear that he had passed away while I was on the world cruise. I met the two of them on an African cruise and I liked her immediately as we stood and chatted at the ship's rail. I really admired her courage and the way she watched over him. His eyesight was failing and she always made sure he didn't miss a step and fall. Now we were both on our own and I wondered to myself if the two of us might team up some time in the future.

It was April when I flew in from London late one evening. When I woke up the next morning, I made myself a cup of tea and looked out the window at the garden. What a sight greeted me! It was like looking at a bulb catalogue. There were the old stalwarts, the King Alfred daffodils, lovely pink narcissi and yellow, white and purple crocuses. The tulips were up but not even the early ones were in bloom just yet. As I looked out I thought of all the hours Colin and I had spent in this garden, planting bulbs and later digging them up to dry and dusting to prevent mildew. We shared a love for gardening and neither of us was afraid of hard work. We could easily spend a whole day working, stopping only for coffee in the morning, lunch and then a tea break in the afternoon. At the end of our labours we'd shower, put on a change of clothes and spend the evening quite happily in front of the TV or reading. Colin would often play his beloved organ while I made dinner. The organ, yes. There was no one to play it now but I knew I couldn't bear to part with it.

That July I had a big birthday party for my sister Betty who was eighty-two. Her birthday was well celebrated because her son and daughter-in-law, Keith and Georgina, invited both of us to their cottage on Murray Lake where we had another party. Betty was already showing signs of Alzheimer's disease. She was forgetful, sometimes even seeming confused about where she was. Even so, she enjoyed the party and being the centre of attention, and didn't seem aware of her own confusion.

Later, in August, my son-in-law, Denny, asked if Tracy, Colin's granddaughter, could be married in my garden. I was thrilled and wanted the garden to be lovely for the big day on September 17th. We decorated the gazebo with ivy and white flowers. Tracy looked radiant in her white gown. I knew that Colin would have been so proud of her.

And, my thoughts went back to our wedding, just a few short years ago in May of 1982. It was also in a garden, Betty and Art's. It was a gorgeous day also. It seemed as if our lives together had gone by so quickly but, until Colin became ill, we filled every day with the joy we found in each other. I hoped Tracy and Sean Ewing would have a long and joyful life together.

Tracy and Sean, a beautiful couple on their wedding day

What makes a good marriage? I've had two wonderful husbands and two that I never should have married. How do you keep the romance alive after the 'falling in love' stage? Is there really such a thing as a soul mate? Here's some short and simple advice from a four time veteran of matrimony. You keep saying you love and appreciate each other and, as an old Scots friend of mine said once "You dress to get him and you dress to keep him."

One day, soon after the wedding, my friend Gladys phoned to ask me if I would be interested in going with her on a BCAA sponsored 'President's' cruise in France.

We would be travelling by riverboat, starting our tour in Lyon, travelling up the Saône River and then down the Rhône into Provence.

"I've been reading all about it, and it sounds relaxing and fun," she said. "It's a great way to see the French countryside without driving or taking a tour bus," she added.

I didn't need much convincing. Colin and I had been on several President's cruises. Essentially they are more expensive than regular tours but, for the higher price you received top notch service, accommodation and meals. They are more personal, as well with more group socializing.

Also, both Gladys and I had first read and then watched the TV version of Peter Mayles' *A Year in Provence*. Provence was definitely on my list of places still to visit. In my mind I could see fields of lavender, sunflowers and poppies. I could almost taste the olives and wine.

"Why not," I answered. I knew we'd have fun and I felt very comfortable about sharing a stateroom with Gladys, which would lower the cost of the trip. I knew she wouldn't fill every available space with cruise wear like the woman from Miami on my world cruise and I also thought that, while Gladys and I would be company for each other, we both would respect each other's need for solo time. I presumed that she felt the same about me. I was right. We proved to be very compatible and have taken several trips together since the first one in France.

We flew to London and then over to Lyons to board the riverboat, the MS Cézanne for an eight day tour. Being aboard the MS Cézanne was a lot like staying in a luxury hotel. Almost everything was provided for us and paid for in advance. However, tipping, alcoholic beverages, telephone calls and laundry were extra as were excursions along the way. Our stateroom was spacious with a large bathroom with marble fixtures and a double sink. We were even given terry towel bathrobes.

Our riverboat, MS Cézanne   *Bedtime*

Working out the morning routine did not prove a problem. I'm an early riser while Gladys likes to sleep in a little. I'd get up, have a shower and dress while she slept and I was out of the way when she got up. I love the early mornings aboard ship. It is quiet on deck, a time for reflection.

Our first stop was Mâcon. Our riverboat tied up at the Quai Lamartine. We had been given an excellent map to guide us as we explored this ancient town on the Saône River. We soon discovered that Mâcon is a city of flowers, with charming squares and small alleyways. A daily vegetable and flower market is held all summer. There was also a traffic-free shopping area in the centre of the town. We had ample time to wander the narrow streets with their ancient stone walls and to visit a church with two mismatched steeples and another one with beautiful stained glass windows. In a side-walk café where we were enjoying mid-morning coffee, looking up high above us, I noticed corn cobs hanging from the rafters! Our guidebook told us that the Saône was the site of the first demonstration of a steam paddle-wheeler. Like many people, I had thought the paddle-wheelers began on the Mississippi.

Flowers in Mâcon

Corncobs drying overhead

That evening our dinner on board featured some of the local produce we had seen earlier at the market; a salad of tomatoes and mesculun, chicken and new potatoes and fruit with fully ripened brie. Drinks were served at the cocktail hour before dinner. The meals on this tour were excellent. There was a breakfast buffet of fruit, eggs, bacon and the best chocolate almond croissants I've ever tasted. Lunch was usually in a restaurant. Dinner provided an opportunity to sample local produce. There was no special seating arrangement which gave us the opportunity to get to know our fellow passengers.

The next morning we were back in Lyon with a full day to explore. We visited the amphitheatre built during the reign of Emperor Augustus. Christian martyrs were fed to lions here in 177 CE.

On our third day we headed down the Rhône River, sitting on deck and enjoying the passing French countryside, Roman ruins and a 16th century castle. We were headed for Montélmar Abbey and then to Glanum on the Via Domita close to St. Rémy de Provence, an area which was inhabited as early as 600 BCE. Via Domita, the ancient Roman road, linked what are now Italy, France and Spain. We visited the Hospice de St. Paul where Van Gogh was a patient for almost a year and where he painted many pictures. The gardens at St. Paul and the chapel and lovely cloisters date back to the 11th century.

Stopping in Viviers, we walked through cobblestone streets to visit the Bishop's palace, the cathedral and the knights' residence, all dating from the 5th century.

Our chef and Glady with desserts

That night we had sailed through dinner and so arrived in Arles for our first day of real exploration in Provence. I read the day's information sheet while Gladys showered, dressed and followed me to breakfast.

Arles was known by the Phoenicians as early as 600 BCE. It was first named Theline and then Arelate, or City of Swamps. The famous amphitheatre, built by the Romans when the city was a metropolis of the Roman Empire in France (Gaul), is in continuous use and regularly filled to capacity. About 100 years B.C.E. it became the site of a canal built by the 6th Legion linking the town with the Mediterranean coast.

Gladys and Margaret, the 'good companions'

The following day our boat tied up in Avignon, the seat of papal controversy in the 4th century. We were looking forward to boarding a bus for a special wine tasting tour of Châteauneuf-du-Pape, the summer residence of the man who declared himself Pope back then. The chateau was beautiful and refreshingly cool. Later we drove to the National Park of the Camargue, set in the marshy delta of the Rhône. Along the way we saw the special small black bulls bred for bull fights, and the white horses said to have been brought to the region by the Saracens, and the pink flamingos at Lake Vaccarès. Late in the afternoon we visited the pilgrimage site of Santes Maries de la Mer, where, according to the gypsies, three saints, all named Marie, arrived from the Holy Land. We said goodbye to our riverboat here and headed by bus down to the Côte d'Azure to Nice and Monaco.

We spent an afternoon in Monte Carlo, which is so well known for its casinos and as a playground for the ultra wealthy. Some of the group visited the casinos but I much preferred to stroll through the town's public gardens. Most of the plants are of the cactus and succulent varieties which require little water in this dry climate. There were flowers everywhere, in hanging baskets, pots and window boxes. I believe that Princess Grace was very instrumental in making Monte Carlo such an attractive place.

That night we were back in Nice for a good-bye party and then on to London where Connie and Ken met us. The flight was nerve racking. There was a storm over the Channel and one of the flight attendants fell into my lap!

Our travels were not over, though. Connie had booked all three of us on a bus trip across the Channel to Paris. The others on the tour were all very congenial; our driver was a real gentleman and our guide, a knowledgeable and pleasant young woman. We arrived quite late in Paris but in time for a bistro meal.

Connie and Gladys left our hotel to buy some milk. When they didn't come back after quite some time, I decided to venture out into the Parisian streets on my own. However, just as I was leaving, an older man from our tour appeared and offered to go with me. We had a pleasant evening together during which time I learned that he had been both a squadron commander and a spy during the Second World War. Connie and Gladys had managed to get lost and only arrived back at the hotel when I did.

Margaret and dinner companion in Paris

Connie and Margaret in Versailles

The next day we all went by the Metro to visit Connie's former au pair girl, Lilo, and her husband, Maurice Lalanne. It was interesting to be invited into a French home and Lilo cooked us a typically French meal; steak with a green pepper sauce made with real cream and a good wine. Thanking them for their hospitality we returned to the underground, this time getting off a stop too early. We had a long walk back to our hotel but who can complain about walking in Paris? We'd be walking more tomorrow, though, because we were off to Versailles.

I had not been back to Versailles since my trip there with Ted in 1957. I knew that anyone planning a trip there should set aside a whole day because Versailles is not just a grand palace, it is also a city and the site of magnificent gardens and parks. Created over three hundred years ago, the estate is vast though no longer consists of the original hunting grounds. Versailles, we learned, is the largest open-air sculpture museum in the world.

We took bread, cheese and fruit with us that day to enjoy a picnic in the very place where Marie Antoinette and Madame Du Barry pretended they were simple country girls instead of the King's wife and mistress.

When we arrived back at our hotel late in the afternoon we were quite worried about my companion of the night before. He had come with us to Versailles but missed the bus back. When we saw him the next morning he told us he wanted to revisit a bar he had frequented during the war and had taken a taxi back to the hotel.

In the morning we all agreed to a boat trip down the Seine past Notre Dame and to visit L'Opéra. A meal in an underground café with a group of chanteuses ended the day in Paris. A bus ride and the Channel ferry took us back to England.

Connie had planned one more outing for us – a trip to the Maldon Salt Flats, where making salt from the saline waters of the Blackwater Estuary has flourished in the area since prehistoric times. That evening she invited friends over for a farewell party. It was farewell to Provence and Paris and time to head home.

Chapter 16

In My Eighties

When Colin knew he was dying he said to me, "We'll live one day at a time, Margaret." It was all we could do.

I still live one day at a time. However, life is different when you are on your own. Some couples who were your friends soon forget you. I was lucky that most of my friends and family have continued to include me in their lives. I will not waste precious moments thinking about those who haven't.

And as difficult as suddenly being on your own is, there are some advantages also. You can plan your day, not having to answer to anyone. You just have to be self-disciplined enough to get up and get going in the morning. I start my day with a cup of tea, which I bring back to bed, followed by a soak in the hot tub. Then, after I shower, dress and eat a simple breakfast, I'm ready to meet whatever challenges the day holds. Every morning my friend, Mary Rochford, calls me on the phone. Not only do I look forward to her cheery call but also I know that if there was anything wrong and if I was unable to answer the phone, she would come over to check on me. There is a real feeling of security in this.

233

A support group can help you come to terms with your grief and will also provide you with a chance to socialize. The one I joined after Colin died is mainly a social group for people who have lost a loved one. A young woman in my bank suggested it to me. It was started by a woman in our local Unitarian Church, Lois Ellis, whose husband was killed in a motorcycle accident. The group met at first to discuss their grief and to view videos which would help them come to terms with their bereavement.

There are, of course, more women than men in the group. Of about twenty-five of us twenty are women and only five men. We meet once every three weeks, usually at night. We go out to dinner or the theatre and also meet for pot luck dinners in one another's homes. We find that conversation isn't easy in restaurants which are often noisy. I have a big house which is ideal for social occasions. In the summer the group comes here for a pool party and they usually come again during the winter.

It is also a good idea to keep busy. Find a new project or become a volunteer. I'm a member of the Eastern Star and roll dressings for cancer patients regularly. Like the support group, volunteering is a good way to meet new friends and forces you to get out and mingle. At the end of the day you return home tired and less likely to dwell on your misfortunes.

Gardening is not only good for the soul; it is good exercise as well. I think I was born with dirt under my fingertips. I'm forever outside deadheading plants, moving things around and checking on my goldfish. Nothing renews your faith in the cycle of life more than seeing the crocuses push up through the earth early in spring.

Travelling, if you can afford it, keeps your mind sharp. I've mentioned my good friend Roy Sommerfield. Roy, in his nineties and an author himself, is still a gallant and romantic man. We've done some travelling together including a recent fourteen day Alaska cruise. He hates to fly so we either have to limit ourselves to cruises originating and ending here in Vancouver or do car trips around the province. We share a room but not a bed. He often takes me out for dinner, frequently at the Yacht Club. He is a gem. I guess I have the best of both worlds; single and in a comfortable relationship with a man I admire.

Travel is also a good way to meet people. I made friends once on a bus en route to Sri Lanka. The bus broke down and we got talking. We soon discovered we had much in common. You just never know when this might happen.

If money is a problem and if working is an option, even a part time job is good for many people. Some women have never had to manage money or even write cheques. Money that you earn yourself can be a good morale booster and can provide the extra funds for travelling.

At age 83 I started to write the story of my life. It was fun and helped me recall all the happy times. I didn't expect to get rich from my writing but I hoped to make enough to cover my expenses. My friend, Roy Summerfield, has also written the story of his life, and we always carry two or three copies of our books when we travel. You would be amazed at the number of times we have sold our books to people we meet. Several times I was sorry I didn't have more copies with me because I could have sold them easily. I've also given copies away; and as mentioned earlier, one even to Queen Elizabeth!

My book has actually received some good publicity, not only in three community newspapers but also in the Vancouver Sun. Sun reporter, Shelly Fralick interviewed me and wrote a lovely article. It is, after all, news when an octogenarian writes a book!

Also, in my first book I wrote about Betty and I being photographed by Gordon Cox. I had kept one of his photographs of me for almost 70 years, not wanting to part with it, while at the same time being afraid to show it to anyone. It was a nude picture taken when I was about 15 years old. Betty and I had earned much needed money posing for Cox. Recently my editor called me to say that there was an exhibition of his pictures at Presentation House Gallery in North Vancouver. "I wonder if your picture is in the exhibit?" she asked.

It was in the exhibit. In fact there were more pictures on display of both Betty and I, taken at the same time. I introduced myself to the curator who invited me to attend the opening of the show that very evening. He was very interested to hear the story behind the photographs. H.G. Cox was considered to be one of the foremost photographers of his time although until his pictures were found in a basement recently, they were all but lost to history. The book that Presentation House published about Cox includes an interview with me as well as the pictures the photographer took of Betty and me.

Recently I returned to my birthplace, Invermere. I was there in 1987 and again in 1991 for a reunion. I took copies of my book for libraries in the Cariboo and Kootenay areas in the province. Books such as mine are often very important tools for people researching local history. I would never have dreamed that my memories of H.G. Cox would appear in a catalogue of his pictures produced for the exhibit. Perhaps if you know the history of your community you could contribute to its record.

I keep a list of everyone who has bought a copy of my book. Most have purchased directly from me but there have been several people from all over the world who have purchased it on line from my publisher, Trafford Publishing.

I'm not any more bashful about promoting my book than I was about advertising my motel in Kamloops. When I owned the Mayfair, if I travelled myself I always told people I was in the motel business and gave them a card with my address and phone number. As a result, we were almost full every night of the year.

I recently came across my guest registry for 1954. The rate was $5.00 per night. Americans were my best customers, coming from as far away as Amarillo, Texas. They came in Mercurys, Packards, Hillmans, Cadillacs and Studebakers. Running the motel was hard work but a lot of fun, too.

After I returned from my world cruise I felt my self confidence returning. I knew I could go it alone and, to be frank, I knew also that I would never marry again. Not that I haven't had proposals, even some in my eighties!

I enjoy my home and garden, love to cook and have friends over for a meal, entertain visitors to Vancouver and show them around my favourite city.

I'm a good cook and good nutrition is one of the things that will keep you well in your own home. Diet and exercise are important every day of your life.

I try to see my sister Betty regularly. She is now in extended care, her dementia having progressed steadily since its onset in 1997. Recently I visited her on her birthday and like the other visits now, it was an ordeal. Five minutes after I've left, she doesn't remember my visit. I don't know why she has Alzheimer's and not me, why I'm enjoying every day and she is so unhappy. We both have had our share of sorrows. Our parents, both our mother and stepmother as well as our father, died while we were still in our teens. Her only daughter, Carol, died in her early twenties and her first husband, Gordon, was killed in a plane crash. I believe she no longer remembers either Carol or Art, her second husband. When I visit I leave feeling that the cheerful and practical Betty I knew is gone, replaced by an unhappy and confused woman. There was always a certain amount of sibling rivalry between us but even that is gone too.

Thanks to Colin's extended family, who have always made me feel one of them, I'm invited to family gatherings and weekends with Lynn and Brett in Whistler and excursions on Denny and Mary's yacht. I also love to stay with them in their condo in Hawaii. It is so peaceful there; I just love to sit and watch the sea where turtles bob up and down lazily. I go for an early walk most mornings and we sometimes drive around the island and have dinner at one of the local restaurants. Family birthdays and special occasions like Christmas, Easter and Thanksgiving, are celebrations in which I'm included.

When I arrived home from Hawaii the last time, after having waited 6 hours in the Honolulu airport, I was met by Lynn and her husband Brett. I was so glad I had dressed nicely for the trip home because they took me directly to the Terminal City Club for lunch. They were celebrating Mothers' Day with Brett's mother, Vi. They always include me, their honorary mother.

I'm also very appreciative of my good friend Mary Rochford, who calls me every morning for a chat. Her "Hi, Margaret, how are you doing?" reassures me that there are many good and caring people in this world.

When friends from far off places come to stay with me I am reminded of the beauty of this province of British Columbia and of Vancouver which has become a very cosmopolitan city. Expo 86 really put us on the world tourist map with visits from important people and heads of state from the world over. I enjoy being a tourist in my own home town, showing off the beaches, parks and mountains as well as the dynamic downtown core and the ethnic areas such as China Town.

If guests stay long enough to explore outside the city, we often go over to Vancouver Island to Butchart Gardens, Little Qualicum Falls and Englishman River Falls. These latter are ideal places for summer picnics. Qualicum Beach is another beauty spot.

Finally, God has a way of helping you to forget the sad times. Remember the Golden Rule; be kind to others and they will generally be kind to you.

ISBN 1-41204755-2

9 781412 047555